The Good Treats Cookbook for Dogs

QUARRY

Peanut Crunch Biscuits, page 78

The Good Treats Cookbook for Dogs

50 HOME-COOKED TREATS
FOR SPECIAL OCCASIONS
PLUS EVERYTHING YOU
NEED TO KNOW TO

Throw a Dog Party!

Barbara Burg

BEVERLY MASSACHUSETTS

QUARRY BOOKS

First published in the United States of America by
Quarry Books, a member of
Quayside Publishing Group
100 Cummings Center
Suite 406-L
Beverly, Massachusetts 01915-6101
Telephone: (978) 282-9590
Fax: (978) 283-2742
www.quarrybooks.com

Library of Congress Cataloging-in-Publication Data
Burg, Barbara.
  The good treats cookbook for dogs : 50 homemade treats for special occasions plus everything you need to know to throw a dog party! / Barbara Burg.
     p. cm.
  Includes index.
  ISBN 1-59253-384-1
  1. Dogs—Food—Recipes. 2. Parties for dogs. I. Title.
  SF427.4.B87 2007
  636.7'085—dc22

2007016595
CIP

ISBN-13: 978-1-59253-384-8
ISBN-10: 1-59253-384-1

9 8 7 6 5 4 3 2 1

Design: Yee Design
Cover Image: Jack Deutsch
Editor: Barbara Bourassa

Printed in Singapore

Contents

Introduction

I have to admit, catering dog parties (actually, that's "pawties") has got to be among the zaniest, funniest, and most enjoyable experiences I have had, paws down—and I've been in professional theater and touring companies while living in New York and Los Angeles. In other words, I've had my share of excitement and memorable good times—but nothing is more celebratory than partying with friends and all of your dogs. Apparently, millions of you agree, given the fact that the pet industry has grown into a multibillion-dollar segment of the economy. Since starting my own doggie bakery, Barbara's Canine Catering, in 1995, I've seen the number of parties increase dramatically each year. We have shipped birthday cakes and party goodies to dogs in every state in the continental United States. Amazing! Our dogs truly are the original "pawty animals"! After all, any moment spent with your dog is cause for celebration.

Whether you have a flair for drama or a desire to keep it simple, everything you need to know to pull off the perfect pup bash can be found in this book. I've included easy-to-prepare recipes, party ideas with lots of style, and hosting tips from sending the invitations to writing thank-you notes. I hope this book—filled with "pawsitively" fun ideas—will inspire you to invite a bunch of your friends and their dogs to get together and celebrate. So let's get our dogs, get in the kitchen, and get this pawty started!

Bone Appetít!

Barbara Burg

CHAPTER 1

Celebrate! Celebrate! Sit, Stay, Drool

Oh boy! We're having a pawty and inviting our dog-loving friends and their dogs. Great! But where do we start? Where should we throw our celebration? How many guests? Should we choose a theme? What do we eat and how much is this going to cost? Relax. Let's tackle one question at a time.

Location, Location, Location

Location is the first decision, as this will set the tone for your party. Your first option for a location is a home with a fenced-in yard. Indoors is fine if you have a tiled area (no carpet!) and only a few small dogs or the space and nerves to handle a larger group. If you opt for the outdoors, make sure that your fence is high enough to restrain any "jumpers" and conditions around the bottom of the fence are secure to thwart any small digging escape artists. Even better, if your yard area is large enough, try to accommodate a play area (even for the most rambunctious guest), an area for food and games, an area for canine parents to relax, and a designated area for canine "relief."

Outdoor areas are ideal for large or small pawties. Typically, a yard area of 30 by 40 feet (9 by 12 m) can host eight to ten dogs. But keep in mind the sizes of the pawty guests. Are the majority of the guests toy breeds, medium-size dogs, or large dogs? Are your guests young and energetic puppies or laid-back seniors? Or does your guest of honor have both small and large buddies or old and young

friends? Keep these questions in mind when selecting your location. If you opt for an outdoor location, consider a backup plan in case of foul weather. Is your garage or indoor area large enough to handle your pawty if it rains? Better yet, include a rain date on your invitation.

The average indoor home area or garage generally can accommodate four or five dogs, keeping in mind the sizes and ages of the guests. But let's not forget about space and seating for the canine parents—you'll need room to party, too. You'll also need to differentiate between the dog treats table and the human refreshment table. Believe me, with the canine spreads that you'll be preparing using this book, it will be difficult to tell them apart.

Whether you opt for indoors or outdoors, here's a checklist to consider for hosting a successful event at your home:

- Select an ample and appropriate area to accommodate whatever size group you're having.

- Arrange for plenty of convenient parking for your guests.

- Tell your neighbors about your dogs' celebration just in case a few guests get yappy. Better yet, invite them over for some canine fun.

- Provide enough "doggie bags" and convenient outdoor trash cans for relief pickup. Be sure to show guests when they arrive the designated "pooping" area and where to find the bags and covered can for those bags. To add a touch of whimsy and make this subject less awkward, personalize a few poop bags for each dog. You may also want to designate someone to perform "poop patrol."

- Remove any items of value that could get in harm's way (or get damaged) when the pawty animals start frolicking.

- Create a comfortable seating area for canine parents to enjoy refreshments and conversation.

- Designate a time-out zone for any canine guest that could use a time-out or a canine attitude adjustment.

- Set up a gift table for the canine guest of honor. Consider displaying a favorite portrait of your dog or a tray or basket of canine pawty favors. How festive!

- Place water bowls throughout the pawty areas. Make sure the water is cool and refilled often. Lots of playing and snacking will certainly make your canine guests thirsty.

So, what if you're not comfortable with the idea of a lot of dogs in your home, or perhaps your pooch's entourage needs a bigger area? Another option to consider is a dog park in your community. Keep in mind that this pawty will be much more casual and less private. Word of a fun dog pawty will spread quickly from dog to dog in the park. Make a sign that says "Pawty Crashers Welcome" and be done with it. Your guests and you will meet more dog parents who will be excited to show off their dog's socialization skills. There is nothing wrong with that.

In order to get all the information that you will need to host a party in a park, you will need to consult with whomever is in charge—a town or city official, the animal control department, an officer of the park, et cetera. Allow plenty of time to book a dog park function, and be sure to check out the local regulations. It's important to find out if all dog guests must show proof of vaccinations, if this an on-leash or off-leash park, and whether there are any other dog-related rules that must be obeyed. Don't forget to include this information in your invitations. The well-informed pawty host, knowing all the dog-park rules, will nip any "pawty fowls and challenges" in the bud.

This is also the time to bring up a few cautionary notes. If hosting your party outdoors, you should note that some flowers and plants are dangerous for dogs. Watch out for chinaberry, azalea, dieffen-bachia, English ivy, daffodil, and wild mushrooms, to name just a few. These can be toxic if ingested by a dog. It's best to consult with your veterinarian about questionable plants and flowers in the area.

With the number of doggie day care and dog training facilities on the rise, these may also be an option. Because your dog is an important member of your family—your canine child, so to speak—these sites play an important role in socialization, training, and general well-being. The facility's manager or "pawty planner" can provide you with all the details, availability, rules, and rental cost. Due to the popularity of dog events, fund-raisers, agility classes, doggie aerobics, and so forth, it's best to get in touch with the facility at least six weeks prior to your event.

Doggie bakeries (or "barkeries") and cafés are also an excellent locale for a "destination" dog pawty. Many dog bark-eries will not only cater the function but will also provide a pawty area and staff to host and move the pawty along. This could also include dog "cleanup," coordinating meet and greet, playing games, passing around yap-paw-tizers, singing "Yappy Barkday," cutting the cake, and pawty cleanup. As a canine caterer, I like this option the best because the guest of honor's canine parents can enjoy their guests and be a part of the soirée, leaving the particulars of the pawty to the pros.

The Guest List

Now that you have chosen (and, if necessary, reserved) your location, let's talk about selecting your canine guests. Not all canines have true pawty potential. Unfortunately, some can be aggressive, territorial, nervous, overbearing, or lacking in basic socialization skills. These guys could spoil all the fun. You can still invite their canine parents, who probably know their dog's limitations, and send mom and dad home with a pawty plate

There is nothing like getting together with a few friends and celebrating a gorgeous summer day at the canine beach.

and a favor bag. If a female dog is in season, you can send her a pawty plate and favor bag as well, as she would unintentionally steal all the attention away from the guest of honor.

Puppies who have had all their vaccinations are perfect pawty guests, and older dogs should be included as well. But, a word of caution ... if you intend to have both older and younger dogs at the same party, be mindful of how the two groups will interact. Of course, older dogs' activity levels are lower. For much of the party, they will probably enjoy lying at their parent's feet after sniffing out the situation. However, younger pups will probably go and go and go until they just about pass out. We all think they're adorable, but the senior dogs may not be so charmed by the puppies' unrelenting enthusiasm. Older dogs will let the younger pups know if they wish to participate in play or not. But I don't recommend letting it get to that point. To avoid potentially agitating the older dogs, designate a puppy play area for the little ones and let them wear themselves out, romping and jumping and rolling all over each other. You can do this with a portable, flexible indoor/outdoor "fence," or with a baby gate (if it's an indoor area), both of which are available at many large online pet retailers.

One fun way to determine if a dog has pawty potential is to invite friends and their dogs to meet at a dog park for a little meet and greet. This is a perfect way to determine who can join in a celebration and who should receive a pawty plate at home.

Choosing a Theme

The next item to consider is theme. Here the possibilities are endless—from simple to craziness itself. Your budget will be a factor. The lower your budget is, the more creative you must be. For any party, two hours is the perfect amount of time, allowing ample time for meet and greet, play, eats, treats, and pawty favors. Be creative and have fun, or take your inspiration from some of my favorite themes:

HAWAIIAN LUAU OR BEACH PAWTY
Very colorful, with beach leis for all guests. Great for any location. If possible,

Simply choose a fun theme and everything else will fall into place. Voila! It's a beach pawty. For Banana Peanut Butter Biscuits, see page 88.

include a kiddie pool filled with water for a refreshing dip. Cookies for humans and dogs can be made in beach-related shapes—boats, fish, lobsters, crabs, beach balls. No party is complete without music. Play all your favorite beach music and Hawaiian-style tunes, and you're sure to have one or two guests show everyone (dogs, too) how to hula dance or limbo.

COWBOY WESTERN THEME Colorful bandanas and cowboy hats for all guests. Cookies shaped like cowboy boots, sheriff's badges, horses, or longhorn cattle would be fun.

GROOVY 1970'S PARTY Tie-dyed bandanas and love beads for all guests. What a fun trip down memory lane to pull out and play all those early '70s tunes. What you serve your human guests should also reflect the theme.

HOLLYWOOD "BLING BLING" AND BLACK TIE AFFAIR Have enough taffeta in assorted colors for all the female guests to wear around their collars, and, of course, black ties for any male canines who leave theirs at home. Music could include your favorite Hollywood movie theme songs. Alternatively, pick a movie and have all dog guests come dressed as their favorite characters—perhaps a character from the *Wizard of Oz* or *Alice in Wonderland,* or even a cartoon character.

FAVORITE NFL, SOCCER/FOOTBALL (OR ANY OTHER SPORT) "PUP" RALLY Team bandanas, hats, and shirts for all guests. Team colors will get the fans cheering. A barbeque or tailgate could be just the thing to get the team spirit going, or serve up football-, soccer-ball-, or helmet-shaped treats.

CELEBRATION OF SPRING OR GARDEN PARTY Ahhh. The sun is out, it's warm, and the flowers are showing off. Time for a party! Cookie shapes can include flowers, butterflies, frogs, or ice-cream cones. Let each guest wear a festive corsage made from artificial flowers on their collar or leash!

BIKER BASH Motorcycle caps, bandanas, and biker clothes for everyone. Motorcycle- or tire-shaped cookie cutters would be fun.

It's not a pawty without a cake. Instead of food coloring, check out a bakery supply shop, and use petal dust. It's non-toxic and natural.

For all themes, keep decorations to a minimum—dogs can have a way of engaging in some destructive fun if there is too much to get into. Specifically, I don't recommend using balloons at a dog party. Sudden and loud noises could frighten the dog guests or, worse, cause a dogfight. Broken balloon pieces could be dangerous, even deadly, if swallowed.

Candles are also not a good idea. Don't use them on the cake or near the dogs' play areas. They can be knocked over by way of a curious dog's nose or a wagging tail. Also, whiskers can be singed or noses burned if they come too close to candles on a cake or table. And you just don't want candles on or near any food items a dog is going to eat, for obvious reasons—a dog won't know what should and what shouldn't be eaten.

Another popular party item to avoid is the noisemaker. The loud and sudden noise from these could frighten or unnerve the dogs and result in unpredictable or undesirable behavior.

Invitation Details

Invitations are a fun and creative way to announce the details of your celebration; inform your guests of any rules (park or beach regulations); set the tone for your bash; and ask for any important information from your guests, such as food allergies. The color, style, and wording will give your guests a taste of your event. Party-supply stores carry a wide variety of invitations, but my dogs and I like to create our own. Stock up on construction paper, dog-related stickers, colored pens, and confetti—the sky's the limit for personalized invitations. Why not purchase a small container of nontoxic water-based paint from an arts-and-crafts store and decorate the invitations with your guest of honor's own paw print? Or enclose a cute picture of the pawty dog and a doggie cookie to tease your guests. Alternatively, many stores that sell scrapbook supplies offer dog-related paper, stickers, quotes, or decorative elements that would make great invitations.

Have fun designing your invitations, and remember that creating your own invitations can be a great children's activity. Don't forget to include the pawty basics:

- Dog of honor's name and dog parents hosting the pawty

- Occasion or reason for your get-together

- Event address; include directions or MapQuest Internet link

- Date, day, and time of your event (if necessary, include a rain date)

- Telephone number and e-mail address for RSVP (This is a must because many dog day cares and bakeries will charge a "per guest" fee, and this information is needed in advance for staffing and for food. You may also need a "please RSVP by" date indicating the cutoff for the final number of guests.)

Invitations should be mailed four to six weeks in advance. Dogs have extremely busy schedules and their social calendars fill up quickly (almost as fast as cats'). When the RSVPs start to arrive, you'll know exactly how much food to prepare or order. You'll also know the number of pawty hats, pawty-favor bags, or game prizes to purchase. After all, what pawty would be complete without games? I like to award prizes for the winners and the "best attempt at winning." Remember that your guests are all winners, and no one should go home with empty paws. Some fun pawty-favor or prize ideas include:

- Dog-themed picture frame

- Gift certificate to a local dog bakery (my personal favorite) or a pet-supply store

- Tennis balls and Frisbees

- Treat bags filled with healthy goodies

- Water bottle with attachable bowl for travel

- Squeaky toys

- Dog charms to attach to their collar

- Gift certificate to a dog spa

As you can see, there are endless creative possibilities for favors and prizes. If you want everyone to feel like a winner, why not make a special keepsake for each guest? You could simply take photos of your dog guests enjoying themselves and send them to the dog parents. These will surely put a smile on every proud parent's face! This also makes an easy thank-you note from your dog to a guest.

And what pawty would be complete without games? Dogs always enjoy a good game, and what better way to burn up a little energy and promote canine and canine parents' bonding than organizing a group activity?

SLOPPIEST KISSER is a favorite. Have your guests call their dogs and make them sit. Then, get your timer ready and have the owners squat down in front of their dogs and instruct them to kiss. Simply see who gets the longest and sloppiest kisses. Time it so that you can announce how long the longest kisser went on. And please have your camera ready! This is great fun—and great bonding—for both the dogs and the dog parents.

TREAT CATCHER is another favorite, especially for the pup. Have your human guests toss a tiny treat to their dogs; the winner is the dog that catches the most airborne treats. Have the owners each stand a designated distance away from their dogs. After each successful toss and catch, have the owners take one large step back, away from their hungry dogs. When the dogs are unable to catch a treat, they are eliminated. The remaining dogs continue to compete until they miss a catch. The owner and dog that can connect from the greatest distance win!

SIT! STAY! is a game that requires great discipline and concentration on your dog's part. Have your human guests instruct their dogs to sit and stay. The winner is the dog that sits the longest. To make the game interesting (and more challenging), try providing different distractions. You can start by walking by with a treat in your hand. This will most definitely eliminate several dogs! Then, you can have the owners step back away from their dogs, or walk in a circle around them, to create another urge to move. If there are still some diehards sitting firmly, bounce or roll a tennis ball by the dogs. You might grab a squeaky toy and squeeze it in front of the dogs. This is a fun exercise and is a good way to test a dog's concentration and work on safety skills, since "Sit! Stay!" can be a critical command in any type of real-life risky situation.

A **FRISBEE TOSS** could be a great outdoor game, especially if you have some agile breeds represented at your party. See whose dog can catch the highest toss or the most tosses in a row. Or perhaps you could have a dachshund race! Or basset waddle, if that's more appropriate! No special course required ... just a starting point and finish line. You can have the owners coax the dachshunds (or other dogs, of course!) along with treats or perhaps a stuffed toy.

One contest that doesn't require any special type of concentration or skill is the **OWNER-DOGGIE DRESS-ALIKE** or look-alike. Just be sure to let the party guests know there'll be a prize for this category, by way of the party invitations. That way, anyone who wants to participate can plan ahead and wear matching bandanas, hair bows, or even theme-related outfits! It's great fun and it definitely creates some hilarious photo opportunities.

In this same vein, you could also have prizes for cutest dog, shortest dog, dog with the longest tail or longest or pointiest ears ... just be creative. If you want, you can come up with categories for everyone, to make sure everyone's a winner and gets a prize.

Sample Pawty Plan

It's usually a good idea to have a rough idea of how you want the party to flow.

The following is a good example for a two-hour event for any type and location:

MEET AND GREET Humans are introduced to each other and leashed dogs are allowed to sniff each other. When your dog guests are comfortable with each other, you can unleash them. Offer the dog parents a homemade treat to reward their dog, and give them a tour of the pawty areas. Be sure to show them the relief area and the disposable bags. This is the time to offer your human guests a beverage, show them the human refreshments, and point out the canine pawty table.

One fun activity for your guests (and something to remember this day with) is a "paw painting." This really brings out the "Pawcasso" in each of our doggies. Visit your local arts-and-crafts store for festive paper and nontoxic water-based paint. Write your dog's name and the date of your soirée on the page. Once a doggie guest is comfortable, simply place a paw in a plate of the paint (you don't need too much paint, just enough to coat a paw pad), place the paper to the paw, and press. Use a paper towel (and water, if needed) to dab off excess paint from the paw, then let the paper dry in an area where the human guests can view and enjoy each other's works of art. Write each dog's name on his or her paw painting in a different color marker. This is also a good time for games.

CELEBRATION CAKE AND PHOTO OPPORTUNITY Have all your guests gather around the guest of honor. The "puparazzi" should get plenty of pictures while everyone is singing "Yappy Barkday" and the birthday dog is enjoying the first licks of the cake.

If you are celebrating a graduation from obedience school, have the photographer get a group photo of all the graduates. Getting all the dogs to sit, stay, and smile pretty for the camera will be an adventure in itself. The moment before the picture is taken, have someone stand behind the photographer and squeeze a squeaky toy or a grunting toy. This will get all the dogs' attention, and voila, you will have a perfect photograph of all the graduates looking at the camera at the same time.

With the group shot complete, it's time to eat the cake. Cut your cake into bite-size pieces. Serve on individual plates with a cookie and a dollop of a muttgarita or your choice of doggie beverage. The bite-size pieces will prevent the "gulpers" from choking on larger pieces. Offer the plates to the dog parents and, allowing plenty of space between the party animals, have them serve their own dogs. Leaving sufficient space between each dog should prevent any food-aggression issues. Be sure to offer seconds by passing a platter of small pieces of cake with cookies, and don't forget the dog drinks.

GIFTS AND PRIZES What's a party without gifts and prizes? This is the time to offer prizes for the various contests you've held—be creative so every dog gets a prize.

While the guest of honor is opening gifts, have a friend keep a list of all gifts and the givers' names. You'll be able to send thank-you notes to the dog guests from your dog and include a photograph of your guests' dogs enjoying the pawty.

Don't forget pawty-favor bags. This can include treats that you prepared for the pawty. You can personalize a treat-bag card that reads, "Thank you for coming to my pawty." Your canine guests will surely leave the pawty with wagging tails and smiles.

Your pawty will be the cat's meow! If it's a small intimate gathering with a dog and a cat, fish-based treats will please them both. Check out the Salmon Yummies on page 34.

CHAPTER 2
Let's Get Baking

When baking treats for dogs, healthy, wholesome, and all natural are key. Fresh ingredients have always influenced the way people eat, and it's no different when it comes to preparing homemade treats for our dogs. Shopping for grains and ingredients at a health food store or in the all-natural section of your favorite supermarket is best. If you enjoy the organic lifestyle, feel free to use organic ingredients in these recipes for your canine companion.

Baking homemade treats for our dog ensures they consume no chemicals, preservatives, fillers, or by-products—you know, the nasty stuff—just healthy grains, fruits, vegetables, herbs, and lean meats. Meats used in commercial treats can contain ingredients from animals identified at the slaughterhouses as one of the four Ds: disabled, diseased, dying, or dead. Because these meats were labeled unfit for human consumption, these animals are released to pet food and treat manufacturers. As far as slaughtered animals go, parts that are considered not fit for human consumption are considered by-products—chicken beaks, feet, ground feathers, et cetera. Clearly these are ingredients we don't want to eat, nor do we want our pets to eat them. When it comes to grains, what is determined to be unfit for human consumption at the milling facility is also allowed in pet foods and treats. These by-products tend to be nothing more than fillers and have little or no nutritional value. With this in mind, there is something to be said about the freshness of a homemade treat and the aroma in the kitchen while it is baking that will keep treat time a happy time. At my house, I don't know who is having more fun, my dogs or me!

Chocolate Is a No-No

On our list of ingredients to avoid is chocolate—a huge no-no. Chocolate can be very toxic to dogs. Dogs cannot break down theobromine, which is found in chocolate. It literally shuts down a dog's system. Baker's chocolate is the most lethal. Milk chocolate is diluted with milk and does not affect a dog's system as quickly. Most important, do not substitute chocolate in recipes that call for carob. Carob is a Mediterranean pod plant that contains no cocoa or caffeine but can be substituted for chocolate in baking. Carob can be purchased in health food stores in chip and powder form.

I also recommend omitting or avoiding sugar, salt, flavorings, and any sauces developed to enhance "people food." Dyes and food coloring are also not necessary. Onions can also cause anemic reactions in some dogs and should be avoided in any homemade treat for your dog. Our faithful companions do not care about color. They want flavor and lots of it!

Some of the cake and biscuit recipes in this book call for baking powder and baking soda. If you don't have these ingredients on hand, however, it's not a problem—without these two leavening agents, the resulting cake or biscuit will be quite dense. Dogs do not need moist and "fluffy." They are, after all, chewing machines. While these treats would give us humans a real jaw workout, our canine friends will enjoy the texture and get more chewing pleasure. Also, if you find a recipe that does include baking powder but you leave it out, keep in mind that the recipe will yield fewer treats.

Other Special Ingredients

Most dogs love fruit, including apples. There are many varieties of apples, including Red Delicious, Golden Delicious, and Granny Smith. These varieties are always reliable and usually readily available. But while you may enjoy the tart flavor of a Granny Smith apple, sour or tart varieties of apples (or other fruits, for that matter) usually are not appealing to dogs. Feel free to experiment with your own dogs to see what they enjoy, but don't be surprised if they don't like those varieties.

As is the case in humans, a small but notable number of dogs appear to be developing allergies to certain foods. Some of the usual suspects include grains, inferior meats or meat by-products, wheat, corn, and soy. Some of this is due to overexposure to certain ingredients over a period of many years, which is one reason why holistic veterinarians recommend rotating your dog's diet periodically to include different meat-protein sources. If you suspect allergies may be a concern with some of your dog guests, include a request on the invitation that asks dog parents to alert you to any possible allergies. That way, you can accommodate any special dietary needs by eliminating those ingredients in the treats you serve. For allergies to wheat, for instance, you can substitute rye flour, and so on.

The recipes formulated in this book are intended as a treat and not as a dog's regular meal. They are designed for the well-being of your dog and to provide a low-fat treat to be added to your dog's diet. If you have any questions or concerns about any ingredients in the recipes, it's always a good idea to consult with your veterinarian. Throughout this book, you will see certain ingredients (fruits, vegetables, nuts) used over and over. That's because the fruits selected in these recipes are favorites of my dogs. Feel free to substitute your pet's favorite vegetables or meats in any of the recipes. After all, we must cater to their every need, want, and desire. And what fun!

To all the great dogs out there about to enjoy a fresh home-baked treat, happy snacking!

Dogs are omnivores. They love meat, fruit, vegetables, flip-flops, socks, armchairs, toilet paper ... you get the picture!

CHAPTER 3

Yap-paw-tizers & Arf-d'oeuvres

What better way to start off your pooch's soirée than serving plenty of doggie-licious yap-paw-tizers? It certainly sets the festive mood and gets those tails wagging. Remember, that's our goal. Working on those socialization skills couldn't be easier when gulping down a tempting, tasty treat.

As guests arrive and introductions are made, it's best to give the dog parents a treat to give their dog. Like any social situation, a dog in unfamiliar surroundings could be a little on guard. After tasting one of these arf-d'oeuvres, even the most tentative guest will be ready to party on. Ask any dog and he'll let you know treats rule.

Salmon Yummies

INGREDIENTS

- one 14 3/4-ounce (420-g) can wild salmon, drained and deboned
- 1 egg, slightly beaten
- 1 carrot, shredded
- 1 tablespoon (4 g) fresh parsley, chopped
- 1 tablespoon (10 g) minced garlic
- 1 cup (30 g) chopped spinach (packed)
- 1/2 cup (115 g) low-fat plain yogurt
- 1 cup (125 g) rye flour
- 1 tablespoon (15 ml) canola oil (or use your favorite oil)

DIRECTIONS

Preheat oven to 375°F (190°C).

Place all ingredients in a medium bowl and mix thoroughly to combine. Refrigerate 1 hour.

Dust hands with rye flour and roll mixture into 1-inch (2.5-cm) balls.

Place balls on lightly greased baking sheet and bake for about 20 minutes or until firm to touch.

Cool and store in a sealed container in the refrigerator. The treats can be made a day ahead of time. Warm in a 375°F (190°C) oven for 10 minutes before arranging on platter.

Do not microwave the treats because microwave ovens heat unevenly and can create hot spots.

■

I prefer to use rye flour in this recipe to accommodate any guests that may have allergies to other flours. You may use wheat flour, if you prefer.

YIELD: 36 balls (depending on size)

All your four-legged guests will sit, stay, and roll over for these Salmon Yummies. And because of the fresh ingredients, don't be surprised if your two-legged guests sneak a taste.

Mugsy says...

If the majority of your friends are small, your parent can roll 1/2-inch (1.3-cm) balls, which will yield more treats! Better yet, ask them to roll assorted sizes and let the dogs decide.

Parmesan Cheese Crisps

INGREDIENTS

- ½ cup (60 g) shredded Parmesan cheese

DIRECTIONS

Preheat oven to 400°F (200°C).

Place 1 heaping tablespoon of Parmesan cheese on parchment paper–lined baking sheet and lightly pat down to form a "cookie."

Repeat with remaining cheese, spacing about ½-inch (1.3-cm) apart.

Bake for 5 minutes or until golden brown.

Cool and store in a sealed container in refrigerator.

YIELD: 8 crisps

Mugsy says...

Be careful: these goodies are quite fragile. To keep them from breaking, ask your parent to place a sheet of wax paper between each layer in the storage container.

"I'm sorry I was busy sniffing around. Did you say cheese?"

Canine Crudités with an Herbal Dip

INGREDIENTS

Herbal Dip

- 1 cup (230 g) low-fat plain yogurt
- 1 garlic clove, minced
- 2 tablespoons (8 g) minced mint
- 2 tablespoons (8 g) minced parsley

Vegetables for Crudités

- 16 green beans with ends snipped
- 16 baby carrots
- 2 small zucchini, cut in half lengthwise, quartered, then cut into 2-inch (5-cm) pieces
- 2 small yellow squash, cut in half lengthwise, quartered, then cut into 2-inch (5-cm) pieces
- 1 sweet potato
- 1 tablespoon (15 ml) canola oil (or use your favorite oil)

Your dog guests will not mind getting their share of vegetables when you offer up this arf-d'oeuvre.

DIRECTIONS

Herbal Dip

Prepare dip by combining yogurt with garlic and herbs. Cover and refrigerate.

Vegetables

Bring 3 quarts (3 liters) water to a boil.

Blanch green beans and carrots for 2 minutes. Remove vegetables with a slotted spoon and place in a bowl filled with ice water. (This stops the cooking process and keeps the vegetables slightly crisp.) Place beans and carrots on a paper towel to drain.

Blanch zucchini and squash in boiling water for 1 minute. Remove vegetables with a slotted spoon and add to ice-water bath. Place zucchini and squash on a paper towel to drain off any excess liquid.

Pierce sweet potato with a fork in several places and microwave on high for 2 minutes. Allow potato to cool, then peel and cut the potato into scant 3-inch (7.6-cm) by 1/2-inch (1.3-cm) sticks. Place in bowl and drizzle with vegetable oil. Store "fries" in a sealed container.

Place a paper towel in the bottom of another container to soak up any liquid and store green beans, carrots, zucchini, and squash in the refrigerator.

To serve, arrange vegetables on a platter along with dip.

YIELD: Serves 8 to 10 dogs

Lift the vegetables out of the water using a slotted spoon.

Spinach Quiche Yap-paw-tizer

INGREDIENTS

- 10 eggs
- ½ cup (60 g) whole wheat flour
- one 10-ounce (280-g) package frozen spinach, thawed and well drained
- ¼ cup (60 ml) vegetable oil
- 2 cups (480 g) low-fat, small curd cottage cheese
- 2 cups (240 g) shredded low-fat cheddar cheese
- 1 cup (120 g) shredded Parmesan cheese

DIRECTIONS

Preheat oven to 375°F (190°C).

In a large bowl, beat eggs. Stir in flour. Stir in spinach, oil, and cheeses. Pour mixture into a 3-quart (3-liter) baking dish and bake for 35 minutes. Remove from oven and let cool 20 minutes before cutting into 2-inch (5-cm) squares.

YIELD: 40 small servings

This recipe is not only perfect for a sleepover, but it is a favorite at Yappy Hour. Leftovers? These quiche bites refrigerate and freeze beautifully.

Mugsy says...

Tell your parent it's very important to drain the spinach before adding it to this recipe. To squeeze out the excess water, your person should place the spinach in a strainer or colander and press a spoon against it.

Puppies will play hard. At the pawty, provide a relaxation area to snooze and get a second wind.

Liver Paté

INGREDIENTS

- 1 pound (454 g) chicken livers
- 3 garlic cloves, minced
- 3 tablespoons (12 g) minced parsley

DIRECTIONS

Bring 6 cups (1.5 liters) water to a boil in a large pot. Add chicken livers. Cover pot and reduce heat to simmer for 15 minutes, or until livers are slightly pink inside. Drain the livers and add to a food processor. Process the livers to a smooth texture.

Transfer to a large mixing bowl, add garlic and parsley, and blend well. Place in a serving bowl, cover, and refrigerate.

Allow the paté to stand at room temperature 30 minutes before serving. Place serving bowl of liver paté on a plate and surround with thin dog biscuits and apple slices.

YIELD. 2 cups (500 g)

For the love of liver! They're begging you to serve them this meaty paté.

Mini Italian Turnovers

No, not rollovers, but turnovers! While the canine kids are frolicking about, heat these little "get the pawty started" yummies and watch your guests "paws" for a treat that is sure to please.

INGREDIENTS

Cheese Filling

- ½ cup (120 g) low-fat ricotta cheese
- ¼ cup (30 g) shredded Parmesan cheese
- 1 tablespoon (4 g) minced fresh parsley

Dough

- 2 cups (250 g) unbleached flour
- ⅛ cup (18 g) cornmeal (white or yellow)
- ½ tablespoon (8 ml) canola oil (or use your favorite oil)
- ¾ cup (175 ml) water

Vegetable Filling

- ¼ cup (20 g) mushrooms, cleaned and sliced
- ¼ cup (20 g) sun-dried tomatoes, well drained of oil, sliced to ⅛-inch (0.3-cm) pieces
- 2 tablespoons (30 ml) milk

DIRECTIONS

Preheat oven to 350°F (180°C).

Grease two baking sheets and set aside.

In a small bowl, stir together ricotta cheese, Parmesan cheese, and parsley and set aside.

In a large bowl, mix all dough ingredients together and knead on a lightly floured surface.

On a lightly floured surface, roll out dough to ⅛- to ¼-inch (0.3- to 0.6-cm) thickness. Cut out 2-inch (5-cm) circles. Place 1 teaspoon of cheese mixture, a slice of mushroom, and a slice of sun-dried tomato on half of each circle of dough. Fold circles in half and seal the edges by pressing firmly with the tines of a fork.

Place the filled turnovers on the prepared baking sheet. Prick the top of each turnover with a fork and brush the tops with milk. Bake for 20 minutes or until golden brown.

Remove turnovers from baking sheet and let cool.

YIELD: 28 turnovers

■

You can continue the Italian theme by serving these delicious treats with a simple tomato dipping sauce. In a small saucepan, combine 1 cup (240 g) tomato purée, 2 minced garlic cloves, and 1½ tablespoons (6 g) chopped fresh parsley. Heat to a boil, reduce the heat, and simmer, covered, for 10 minutes. Cool slightly and serve alongside the turnovers.

Getting together with a big group of dogs provides a great opportunity to learn all about the beautiful breeds, from the common to the uncommon.

Mugsy says...

You can use any filling we like for these turnovers. My favorites include ground turkey, ground beef, ground chicken, shredded carrots, or wilted spinach. Pamper us with our favorites!

Peanut Butter Cheese Dip

INGREDIENTS

- 8 ounces (230 g) cream cheese, softened to room temperature
- ½ cup (130 g) all-natural crunchy peanut butter
- 1 Red or Golden Delicious apple
- ⅛ cup (30 ml) lemon juice

DIRECTIONS

Using a hand mixer, combine cream cheese and peanut butter. Blend well.

Cut the apple in half, then scoop out the seed area and discard. Divide the remaining apple into 12 wedges. To prevent the wedges from turning brown, give them a lemon-juice bath. Scoop out cheese mixture with melon baller or small spoon and place in center of apple wedge.

To serve, arrange on a platter with any leftover dip.

YIELD: 1 cup (250 g)

An apple a day could keep the vet away. Adding the peanut butter and cream cheese dip makes the "medicine" go down.

Salmon Arf-d'oeuvres

This luscious "yap" will certainly set the tone, and canine guests will know that this pawty is no ordinary "arf-fair."

INGREDIENTS

- 14 3/4-ounce (420 g) can wild salmon, drained and deboned
- 1 stalk celery, finely minced
- 1/2 cup (115 g) low-fat plain yogurt
- 1 tablespoon (4 g) chopped fresh parsley
- 2 garlic cloves, minced
- spinach leaves (optional)

DIRECTIONS

Place all ingredients in a medium bowl and mix thoroughly to combine. Add more yogurt for a creamier mixture, if desired.

On a serving plate, pat the mixture into the shape of a fish.

Refrigerate 1 hour.

Serve with biscuits of the day. This spread also tastes great on Parmesan Cheese Crisps (page 32).

YIELD: 18 to 20 servings

Mugsy says...

If your party will have a theme, your parent can vary the shape of this cake to match. Lining the mold with plastic wrap allows easy removal to the serving plate and helps hold the shape. For added color, line the plate with spinach leaves.

Our canine friends don't just crave food and treats. They crave exercise. No, that's not a salmon.

Salmon Loaf with Sweet Potato Rounds

INGREDIENTS

- 14 3/4-ounce (420 g) can wild salmon, drained and deboned
- 1 tablespoon (10 g) minced garlic
- 2 tablespoons (8 g) dried oregano, divided
- 2 tablespoons (8 g) chopped fresh parsley, divided
- 1 egg, slightly beaten
- 1/2 cup (65 g) rye flour
- 1 cup (30 g) chopped spinach (packed)
- 2 large sweet potatoes

DIRECTIONS

Bake sweet potatoes at 425°F (220°C) for 25 minutes and let cool.

Peel and slice the potatoes into 1/4-inch (0.6-cm) rounds and set aside.

Combine salmon, garlic, 1 tablespoon (4 g) oregano, 1 tablespoon (4 g) parsley, egg, flour, and spinach in a large bowl. Chill for 1 hour.

Preheat oven to 400°F (200°C).

Mix remaining oregano and parsley together on a sheet of wax paper. Roll the salmon mixture into four 4-inch (10-cm) by 1-inch (2.5-cm) loaves. Roll loaves in herbs. Place on a lightly greased baking sheet and bake 20 minutes.

Cool and store in a sealed container in the refrigerator.

To serve, slice the salmon loaf into 1/4-inch (0.6-cm) slices and place on top of sweet potato rounds.

YIELD: 60 salmon slices and 20 potato rounds

Here fishy, fishy, fishy. These scrumptious salmon treats taste great teamed up with sweet potato rounds for a dog-friendly and healthy version of fish and chips. They are also yummy with Parmesan Cheese Crisps (page 36).

Mugsy says...

Freeze any leftover salmon loaves and use as a food topper or individual treats.

Biscotti

Biscotti is enjoyed the world over. And guess what? Dogs love these crunchy treats as well!

INGREDIENTS

- ¼ cup (65 g) all-natural peanut butter
- ½ cup (115 g) puréed pumpkin
- ¼ cup (60 g) canola oil (or use your favorite oil)
- ½ cup (120 ml) water
- 2 eggs, slightly beaten
- 2 tablespoons (27.6 g) baking powder
- 4 cups (500 g) whole wheat flour
- ½ cup (90 g) carob chips, unsweetened

DIRECTIONS

Preheat oven to 350°F (180°C). Lightly grease a baking sheet or biscotti pan.

In a large bowl, combine peanut butter, pumpkin, and oil. Add water and eggs and mix well. In a medium bowl, sift together baking powder and flour.

Add flour mixture to the peanut butter mixture and mix well. Fold in carob chips and turn onto a lightly floured surface.

Knead dough, then form into a 15 x 4 x 1½-inch (38 x 10 x 4-cm) loaf. If you are using a biscotti pan, shape the dough and flatten in the pan. Bake for 50 minutes. Cool on a wire rack.

With a sharp knife, cut the loaf into ¼-inch (0.6-cm) slices and place on a lightly greased baking sheet. Bake for 10 additional minutes.

Cool and store in a sealed container in the refrigerator.

YIELD: 28 to 30 individual biscotti

"I don't know about you, but I'm thinking about a pumpkin biscotti right about now ... and it wouldn't hurt to spread a little peanut butter on it."

CHAPTER 4

Pawty Pleasers

The pawty is in full swing. Dogs and their humans are chomping on treats. The music is playing and your dog's entourage is frolicking about. It's all about the sniffing, socializing, and playing games. Meanwhile, you continue to check human beverages, refill dog water bowls, and serve delicious treats. All platters of treats—whether human or canine—are positioned on the tables out of reach of any canine counter surfers.

Decorating the canine treat table with dog toys, dog photos, and dog-bone place cards identifying each canine goodie will inform guests that treats on this table are "going to the dogs." Let's bring out our second round of treats. These unique, delectable treats will ensure everyone will be yapping about your party.

Turkey Medallions with Dipping Sauce

INGREDIENTS

Dipping Sauce

- 1 cup (230 g) low-fat plain yogurt
- 2 tablespoons (8 g) minced mint

Turkey Medallions

- 1 pound (450 g) ground turkey
- 2 eggs, slightly beaten
- 1 cup (30 g) chopped spinach (packed)
- 2 tablespoons (8 g) minced parsley
- 1 tablespoon (4 g) minced mint
- 2 garlic cloves, minced
- 1½ cups (120 g) whole rolled oats
- 1 cup (125 g) rye flour
- ¼ cup (30 g) shredded Parmesan cheese
- 1 tablespoon (15 ml) canola oil (or use your favorite oil)

DIRECTIONS

For the dip, stir yogurt and mint in small mixing bowl to blend. Cover and refrigerate.

Gently mix turkey with all remaining ingredients in a medium bowl. Form mixture into 2-inch (5-cm) patties for larger dogs and 1-inch (2.5-cm) patties for smaller dogs.

Prepare barbeque grill and preheat to medium high. Grill patties until thoroughly cooked, about 4 minutes per side, depending on patty size.

Place on platter and serve with mint sauce. Patties can be served drizzled with sauce or can be individually dipped.

YIELD: 36 to 42 medallions (depending on size)

A great game of Red Rover, Red Rover could come to an abrupt stop when serving these grilled turkey medallions with yogurt mint sauce.

Mugsy says...

We enjoy grilling just as much as people do. If the outdoor weather is not cooperative for grilling, your person can prepare these medallions on a stove. Simply heat canola oil in a skillet on medium high, then sauté patties for 3 to 4 minutes per side.

Veggie Bites

Here's another "sneaky" way to ensure that our pawty animals get their "minimum" daily requirement of vegetables. If only they could talk. They would say, "Yummmmm." Keep the drool to a minimum and serve these quickly.

INGREDIENTS

Small Biscuits

- 2 cups (250 g) unbleached flour
- 2 teaspoons (9.2 g) baking powder
- ¼ cup (50 g) vegetable shortening
- ⅔ cup (150 ml) milk

Filling

- 8 ounces (230 g) cream cheese, softened to room temperature
- ¼ cup (8 g) frozen spinach, thawed and well-drained
- ½ cup (30 g) shredded carrots
- 2 garlic cloves, minced
- 1 tablespoon (4 g) fresh parsley, finely minced

DIRECTIONS

Preheat oven to 425°F (220°C).

Small Biscuits

Lightly grease a baking sheet.

Sift flour and baking powder into a bowl. With a pastry blender, cut shortening into flour. It will be crumbly. Add milk and work into a dough. Mix well and knead dough on a lightly floured surface until thoroughly mixed.

On a lightly floured surface, roll out dough to ½-inch (1.3-cm) thickness. Cut out 1½-inch (3.8-cm) circles with a cookie cutter or small glass.

Place biscuits on a greased baking sheet.

Filling

Mix all ingredients well. Mound a generous portion (don't skimp) on top of biscuit dough circles. Bake for 15 minutes. Cool on a rack before serving.

Serve immediately or store treats in a sealed container in refrigerator.

YIELD: About 35 biscuits

Don't forget to take the group photograph of all your pawty animals. Remember the moment.

Mixed Grill

Want to add flavor to this recipe? Make the brown rice with homemade chicken stock.

INGREDIENTS

Brown Rice Prepared with Homemade Chicken Stock

- 1 cup (190 g) store-bought, salt-free brown rice
- 2 cups (475 ml) homemade chicken stock (do not use canned stock; see tip, page 57)

Mixed Grill

- 1 boneless, skinless chicken breast half, pounded to ¼-inch (0.6 cm) thickness
- 2 tablespoons (30 ml) canola oil (or use your favorite oil), divided
- 1 tablespoon (4 g) dried oregano, divided
- 2 garlic cloves, minced, divided
- Two 4-ounce (60 g) salmon filets
- one 8-ounce (110 g) rib eye steak
- ¼ cup (30 g) shredded carrots for garnish (optional)

DIRECTIONS

Brown Rice

Prepare rice following package instructions (do not add salt) but substitute homemade chicken stock for water. Store in airtight container in refrigerator.

Mixed Grill

Marinate chicken in 1 tablespoon (15 ml) oil, half of the oregano, and half of the garlic for 30 minutes. Prepare grill (medium-high heat). Grill chicken until just cooked through, about 6 minutes per side. Transfer chicken to cutting board and let rest 5 minutes.

Brush salmon with oil. Grill salmon until just opaque in center, about 4 minutes per side. Transfer salmon to cutting board and let rest for 5 minutes.

Marinate rib eye in 1 tablespoon (15 ml) oil and remaining half of the oregano and garlic for 30 minutes. Grill rib eye about 5 minutes on one side and 4 minutes on the other. Transfer to cutting board and let rest 10 minutes.

To serve, heat rice. Press into lightly oiled ¼-cup measuring cup (or soufflé cup) and place on plate.

Slice chicken, steak, and fish into ¼-inch (0.6-cm) slices or bite-size pieces.

Arrange slices around rice mound and garnish with a bit of shredded carrot.

YIELD: Serves up to 10 dogs

It could be difficult to prevent human guests from eating this treat. Mixed Grill always gets the "high paw" reaction from all party animals.

Here's the bad news: commercial, canned chicken stock often contains salt and onions, and onions are on the no-no list for canines. But here's the good news: it's easy to make your own chicken stock. Place a cut-up (raw) chicken (back and neck included), two whole carrots, two celery stalks, 1 tablespoon (4 grams) chopped parsley, and two chopped garlic cloves in a large Dutch oven or pot. Cover with water and bring to a boil. Cover pot and simmer for 30 minutes. Turn off heat. Lift out pieces of chicken and vegetables with slotted spoon. Reserve for later use. To strain, pour stock through a sieve. Freeze in 1 cup (235 ml) containers for later use.

Walnut Carob Bonbons

INGREDIENTS

- 1 cup (200 g) vegetable shortening
- 1 teaspoon (5 ml) vanilla
- ¾ cup (115 g) walnuts, finely chopped
- 2 ¾ cups (345 g) unbleached flour
- ½ teaspoon (2.3 g) baking powder
- 1 cup (180 g) carob chips, unsweetened
- 1 tablespoon (15 ml) canola oil (or use your favorite oil)

DIRECTIONS

Preheat oven to 325°F (170°C).

In a large mixing bowl, cream shortening with a beater. Add vanilla, mixing well. Fold in walnuts.

In a medium bowl, combine flour and baking powder. Add the flour mixture to the shortening and beat until well blended.

Roll pieces of dough into 1-inch (2.5-cm) balls. Place balls on *ungreased* baking sheet.

Bake for 15 minutes. Cool the balls on wire racks.

Place the carob in a microwavable dish and stir in oil. Cook the carob at 50 percent power for 1–2 minutes, until softened, then stir until smooth. Gently dip bonbons into melted carob and sprinkle with walnuts.

Store layered between sheets of wax paper in an airtight container.

YIELD: 30 bonbons

■

This recipe can also be made with finely chopped, unsalted peanuts. Remember that variety is the spice of life.

Mugsy says...

If your friends are smaller dogs, adjust the size of these bonbons. A variety of sizes will accommodate everyone from a Chihuahua to a Great Dane.

Agility courses are easy to set up and provide hours of entertainment. They can be purchased online or at most pet supply stores.

Vegetarian Pizza

INGREDIENTS

Pizza Crust

- 4 cups (500 g) unbleached flour
- ¼ cup (35 g) cornmeal (white or yellow)
- 1 tablespoon (15 ml) canola oil (or use your favorite oil)
- 1 ½ cups (350 ml) water

Pizza Topping

- ½ cup (120 g) tomato purée (no added salt or sugar)
- 1 tablespoon (10 g) minced garlic
- 2 tablespoons (8 g) chopped fresh parsley, divided
- ¼ cup (30 g) shredded Parmesan cheese

DIRECTIONS

Preheat oven to 300°F (150°C).

Pizza Crust

Mix all pizza crust ingredients together in a large bowl.

Knead dough on a lightly floured surface. Roll out dough and cut out 2- or 3-inch (5- or 7-cm) circles or squares using a pizza cutter or sharp knife.

Lightly oil a baking sheet and sprinkle with a dusting of cornmeal. Place crusts on sheet and pierce crusts with a fork to prevent bubbles.

Bake for 25 minutes.

Pizza Topping

Mix tomato purée, garlic, and 1 tablespoon parsley until blended. Spread the mixture evenly over the cooled pizza crusts. Sprinkle with a pinch of parsley and a pinch of Parmesan cheese.

Bake for 15 minutes.

Cool and store in sealed container in refrigerator.

YIELD: 55 to 65 (depending on size)

Who doesn't like pizza? Watch the puppies, teenagers, and senior dogs alike all gather around the pizza plate. Belissimo!

Swedish Turkey Balls

This is truly a traditional Scandinavian delight. This recipe doubles perfectly, so you can freeze some for later.

INGREDIENTS

- 1 pound (450 g) ground turkey
- 1 cup (115 g) fine, dry bread crumbs
- ¼ cup (60 ml) milk
- 1 egg
- 2 tablespoons (8 g) minced parsley
- 2 garlic cloves, minced
- 2 tablespoons (30 ml) canola oil (or use your favorite oil), adjust quantity if needed
- 4 ounces (115 g) sour cream
- 2 tablespoons (8 g) unbleached flour
- 1 cup (235 ml) water

DIRECTIONS

In a large bowl, stir together turkey, bread crumbs, milk, egg, parsley, and garlic. Mix well. Roll the mixture into approximately 40 to 45 1-inch (2.5-cm) balls.

In a 10-inch (25-cm) skillet, heat oil. Fill skillet with meatballs and cook 12 minutes, turning meatballs to brown evenly. Remove meatballs to a plate and set aside. Add remaining meatballs to skillet and repeat.

In a small bowl, combine sour cream and flour. Add water, mixing well. Stir the mixture into the drippings remaining in the skillet. Heat until the gravy is thickened and bubbly.

Add meatballs to the gravy in the skillet and heat thoroughly.

Cool and garnish with additional chopped parsley before serving.

YIELD: 40 to 45 balls

"If I concentrate really hard, maybe that ball will turn into a Swedish Turkey Ball."

Mini Meat Loaf with Tomato Herb Sauce

INGREDIENTS

Meat Loaf

- 1 pound (450 g) ground turkey or low-fat beef
- 1 cup (30 g) chopped spinach (packed)
- ½ cup (60 g) shredded carrots
- 3 eggs
- 2 tablespoons (8 g) chopped fresh herbs (thyme, basil, mint, parsley, or any of your dog's favorites)
- 2 cups (160 g) whole rolled oats
- 2½ cups (310 g) whole wheat flour
- ¼ cup (60 ml) canola oil (or use your favorite oil)

Sauce

- 1 cup (245 g) tomato purée (no added salt or sugar)
- 2 tablespoons (8 g) dried oregano
- 2 garlic cloves, minced
- 2 tablespoons (8 g) chopped fresh parsley

DIRECTIONS

Preheat oven to 350°F (180°C).

Meat Loaf

Mix turkey, spinach, and shredded carrots in a large bowl.

In another bowl, combine eggs, herbs, oats, wheat flour, and oil. Add this mixture to turkey and blend well. Place in lightly oiled 6 x 3 x 2-inch (15 x 8 x 5-cm) pans and bake for 30 minutes. Check for doneness with a knife.

Let cool and then slice into individual servings. Serve on a platter with the Tomato Herb Sauce.

Sauce

Combine tomato purée, oregano, garlic, and parsley until well blended.

Pour into serving dish and refrigerate.

YIELD: 4 loaves

Mugsy says...

I love these so much, I ask my mom to make some extra— these loaves can be frozen for up to two months.

Who said meat loaf has to be boring? Evidently they didn't try this loaf. Pass the tomato herb sauce, please.

Peanut Butter Barkfast Bars

These are soooo yummy. Does this recipe go on the dog or the human table? Why not both?

INGREDIENTS

- 4 cups (400 g) oat cereal flakes
- ¾ cup (60 g) whole rolled oats
- ½ cup (60 g) unbleached flour
- ½ cup (75 g) dried apples, diced
- ¼ cup (30 g) dried cranberries
- 2 eggs, slightly beaten
- ¼ cup (55 ml) honey
- ⅓ cup (85 g) all-natural peanut butter
- ¼ cup (60 ml) vegetable oil

DIRECTIONS

Preheat oven to 325°F (170°C).

Lightly grease a 9 x 9 x 2-inch (23 x 23 x 5-cm) baking pan.

In a large bowl, combine cereal, oats, flour, apples, and dried cranberries and set aside.

In a medium bowl, combine eggs, honey, peanut butter, and oil.

Pour peanut butter mixture into cereal mixture and mix well. Pour mixture into pan and bake for 30 minutes.

Cool on a wire rack before serving.

When ready to serve, cut into bars using a serrated knife.

YIELD: About 32 to 35 bars

"Has anyone ever told you that you look like a Peanut Butter Barkfast Bar?"

Sushi Roll

INGREDIENTS

Sushi Rice

- 3 cups (705 ml) water
- 1 cup (100 g) short grain sushi rice

Sushi Roll

- 1 cup (100 g) prepared sushi rice
- 2 sheets nori
- 1 tablespoon (8 g) toasted sesame seeds (optional)
- 2 rolls imitation crab (or substitute chicken strips)
- ½ avocado, cut into strips
- ¼ cup (30 g) shredded carrots (use more for garnish, optional)
- canola oil (or use your favorite oil) for light drizzle

Wow! These little yummies are sure to please. The choices of filling ingredients are endless . . . and you don't have to let them know that this treat is a healthy one.

DIRECTIONS

Sushi Rice

Place water in a medium saucepan. Cover and bring to a boil. Reduce heat to simmer. Add rice, return to boil, and reduce heat to simmer. When the water has evaporated, remove pan from heat. Cool rice before using.

Sushi Roll

Place one sheet of nori lengthwise on a bamboo mat, shiny side down. Position the sheet about 1 inch (2.5 cm) from the side of the mat closest to you.

Place a handful of sushi rice in the center of the nori and gently spread evenly across. Wet hands with water to make this step easier.

Sprinkle sesame seeds on rice. Place a strip of crab (or chicken), an avocado strip, and carrots horizontally across the roll. Drizzle a little oil on the crab, avocado, and carrots.

Use the mat to roll up the sushi, squeezing the mat to shape it into a cigar shape.

Repeat with second sushi roll.

Wrap the rolls and refrigerate until ready to serve.

Before serving, use a sharp knife to slice rolls into 1-inch (2.5-cm) -thick pieces.

Serve on a platter with rice side facing up and garnish with shredded carrots.

YIELD: Serves up to ten dogs

■

The possibilities for a variety of sushi are endless. Again, use your pooch's personal preferences.

Sleep Over Benedict

This treat is a bit involved in preparation, but the results are well worth it!

INGREDIENTS

- 4 slices turkey bacon
- 4 English muffin halves
- 1 teaspoon (5 ml) vinegar
- 4 eggs
- 1 cup (30 g) spinach

DIRECTIONS

In a nonstick skillet, sauté the turkey bacon following the package directions.

Break bacon in half, place on a plate, and keep warm.

Toast English muffins until golden.

In a large skillet, bring 2 inches (5 cm) of water and the vinegar to a boil. Crack one egg into a small glass or cup. Reduce heat to simmer and pour egg into water. Add remaining eggs, cracking each one into a small glass or cup and pouring it quickly into the water.

Let eggs cook 4–5 minutes.

Using a slotted spoon, remove the eggs and drain on a paper towel.

In a small skillet, bring ¼ cup (60 ml) of water to a boil. Reduce heat to simmer and add spinach. Cook until all water has evaporated, being careful not to burn the spinach.

To assemble Eggs Benedict, top each muffin with spinach, two pieces of bacon, and a poached egg.

YIELD: 4 servings

This is not an ordinary morning! This is the stuff that doggies dream of. Puppy-dog tails will get a-waggin' when pooches come into the kitchen and see this on their plate. Goooood morning.

Cheesy Cheese Pizza

You just may be likely to try one of these yourself. Don't let your pooch see you.

INGREDIENTS

Pizza Crust

- 2 cups (250 g) unbleached flour
- ⅛ cup (17 g) cornmeal (white or yellow)
- ½ tablespoon (7 ml) canola oil (or use your favorite oil)
- ¾ cups (175 ml) water
- oil for brushing

Pizza Topping

- 4 ounces (115 g) shredded mozzarella cheese
- 2 ounces (56 g) crumbled goat cheese
- ¼ cup (60 g) part skim ricotta cheese
- 2 tablespoons (10 g) freshly grated Parmesan cheese
- 2 tablespoons (8 g) chopped fresh oregano

DIRECTIONS

Preheat oven to 350°F (180°C).

Pizza Crust

Mix all pizza crust ingredients together in a large bowl.

Knead dough on a lightly floured surface. Roll out dough and cut out 2- or 3-inch (5- or 7-cm) circles or squares using a pizza cutter or sharp knife.

Lightly oil a baking sheet and sprinkle with a dusting of cornmeal. Place crust circles or squares on baking sheet and pierce crusts with a fork to prevent bubbles. Lightly brush crusts with oil.

Bake for 25 minutes.

Pizza Topping

In a medium bowl, mix the four cheeses together.

Top the pizza rounds or squares with the cheese mixture, leaving ⅓-inch (0.4-cm) plain border. Top with chopped oregano.

Bake pizza until cheese melts, about 15 minutes.

Transfer to serving platter and serve slightly warm to touch.

YIELD: 56 to 58 pizzas

If you don't have a pizza cutter, a knife will do the trick for pizza squares. A plastic drinking glass will work beautifully for pizza circles.

CHAPTER 5

More Cookies, Please

When it comes to food, some of your guests may have possessive tendencies, and if you're not careful, the festivities can become a free-for-all. It is the responsibility of each parent to be aware of his or her own dog's whereabouts and behavior. Never allow dogs to share treats from the same plate, and discourage any exploring, uninvited nibbling, or an innocent sniff of another dog's plate by keeping sufficient space between each guest.

Chances are everyone will want to try a taste of everything served, so I recommend keeping portions small. I think moderation and portion control are key. Keep all perishable party arf-d'oeuvres in the refrigerator until ready to serve, and keep plenty of clean, fresh water available to quench doggie thirst. With this in mind, it's time to spice things up with "more cookies, please."

Apple Kissed Peanut Butter Treats

INGREDIENTS

Cookies

- ½ cup (125 g) unsweetened applesauce
- 1 large egg
- ½ cup (130 g) peanut butter
- 1½ cups (355 ml) water
- 4 cups (500 g) whole wheat flour
- ½ cup (70 g) cornmeal (white or yellow)
- ¾ cup (60 g) whole rolled oats

Filling

- 8 ounces (230 g) cream cheese softened to room temperature

DIRECTIONS

Preheat oven to 325°F (170°C).

Combine applesauce, egg, peanut butter, and water in a large bowl.

Combine dry ingredients in a separate bowl. Add dry ingredients to applesauce mixture. Mix well, then knead dough on a lightly floured surface until thoroughly mixed.

Roll dough to ⅛-inch (3-mm) thickness, and cut out shapes using cookie cutters.

Place on a lightly greased cookie sheet and bake for 50 minutes. Turn oven off and leave biscuits in oven for 20 minutes to harden. Transfer to rack and cool completely.

When biscuits have cooled, spread cream cheese on a cookie and top with another cookie, pressing together lightly.

Store treats in a sealed container in refrigerator.

YIELD: 60 treats (yielding 30 sandwiches)

Mugsy says...

If your parents choose a specific theme for your party, ask them to use cookie-cutter shapes to complement the theme. If your friends are small and large, ask your parents to vary the size of the cookie cutters.

Get starstruck with these yummy "apps" and watch the puparazzi go wild.

Peanut Crunch Biscuits

INGREDIENTS

Cookie

- 1 cup (250 g) wheat germ
- 3 cups (375 g) whole wheat flour
- ½ cup (40 g) whole rolled oats
- 1 cup (260 g) all-natural crunchy peanut butter
- 3 tablespoons (45 ml) canola oil (or use your favorite oil)
- 1 egg
- 1 cup (235 ml) water

DIRECTIONS

Preheat oven to 300°F (150°C). Adjust rack to the lower third of the oven.

Combine wheat germ, flour, and oats in a bowl. Add peanut butter, canola oil, egg, and water. Mix all ingredients together. (You may find it easier to knead the mixture with your hands.)

On a lightly floured surface, roll out dough to ¼-inch (0.6-cm) thickness and cut into desired shapes with cookie cutters. Repeat rolling and cutting out all dough until completely used.

Place on lightly greased baking sheet and bake 40 minutes. Turn off oven but leave biscuits inside until crunchy, at least 1 hour.

Store in sealed container.

YIELD: 50 to 60 biscuits (depending on size of cookie cutters)

■

Most health-food stores provide machines that can grind whole peanuts in any amount needed. I recommend this step, as commercial peanut butters contain sugars, salt, and BHA preservatives designed for human taste buds, not doggies.

The cowboy western theme comes to life serving up cookies in these fun shapes. No dog would mind doing a giddyup and riding the range for these biscuits.

Mugsy says…

Sealed containers help keep moisture out. Moisture is our biscuits' worst enemy to long shelf life since it promotes growth of mold. All of these recipes are all natural, meaning that they omit preservatives and chemicals that prevent mold. Be sure to store products in a cool, dry place or better yet, ask your parent to store them in the refrigerator.

Pumpkin Twists

INGREDIENTS

- 1 cup (235 ml) water
- 1 tablespoon (15 ml) canola oil (or use your favorite oil)
- 2 eggs, slightly beaten
- ¼ cup (60 g) puréed pumpkin
- 3 cups (375 g) whole wheat flour
- 3 cups (375 g) unbleached flour
- 1 cup (140 g) cornmeal (white or yellow)

DIRECTIONS

Preheat oven to 300°F (150°C).

In a large bowl, combine water, oil, eggs, and pumpkin.

In a second bowl, combine flours and cornmeal.

Add the dry ingredients to the wet ingredients and mix thoroughly until well blended.

On a lightly floured surface, roll out dough to ¼-inch (0.6-cm) thickness. With a knife or pizza cutter, cut out strips 4 inches (10 cm) long and ½ inch (1.3 cm) wide. Twist strips and place on a greased baking sheet.

Bake for 30 minutes. Turn off oven and let cool inside oven for 30 minutes.

Cool and store in a sealed container.

YIELD: About 50 twists

■

Did you know that pumpkin is high in digestible fiber? If your dog has a bout with diarrhea, spoon a little pumpkin on his or her food. It works like a charm. To prevent losing pumpkin to mold, simply place spoonfuls on a flat surface (i.e., cutting board) large enough to fit in your freezer. After the pumpkin freezes, place all the mounds in an airtight resealable plastic bag. Keep frozen until needed and use one at a time.

With these goodies, your dog will twist the night away. These treats are also perfect for training bits. They break easily for each sit, stay, and drool.

Chicken Ginger Biscuits

INGREDIENTS

- 2 cups (250 g) whole wheat flour
- ½ cup (125 g) wheat germ
- 1 tablespoon (5 g) ground ginger
- ½ cup (120 ml) chicken broth
- 1 egg, slightly beaten
- ¼ cup (60 ml) vegetable oil

DIRECTIONS

Preheat oven to 375°F (190°C).

In a medium bowl, combine flour, wheat germ, and ginger.

In a second bowl, combine chicken broth, egg, and oil. Add the dry ingredients to the wet ingredients and mix until well blended.

On a lightly floured surface, knead the dough and roll out to ¼-inch (0.6-cm) thickness. Using cookie cutters, cut into desired shapes. Combine dough scraps and repeat rolling and cutting into biscuits until all dough is used.

Place biscuits on a greased baking sheet and bake for 25 minutes.

Cool on a rack before serving.

Store biscuits in a sealed container.

YIELD: About 36 large or 60 small biscuits

■

Dogs enjoy the flavor of ginger. Ginger can also be helpful in aiding digestion: it will relieve an upset tummy and ease motion sickness.

"Go ahead … call me chicken; just don't call me late for supper!"

Banana Peanut Butter Biscuits

INGREDIENTS

- 2 cups (250 g) unbleached flour
- 1 cup (125 g) whole wheat flour
- $\frac{1}{2}$ cup (70 g) cornmeal (white or yellow)
- $\frac{1}{4}$ cup (35 g) nonfat dry milk
- $\frac{3}{4}$ cup (60 g) whole rolled oats
- 1 egg, slightly beaten
- $\frac{1}{2}$ mashed banana
- $\frac{1}{2}$ cup (130 g) all-natural crunchy peanut butter
- $1\frac{1}{2}$ cups (350 ml) water

Set the tone for your party with fun cookie-cutter shapes. Set sail on a beach theme with lobsters, crabs, sailboats, and other nautical shapes.

DIRECTIONS

Preheat oven to 350°F (180°C).

Combine all dry ingredients in a large bowl.

Add the egg, banana, and peanut butter and blend well. Add water gradually, kneading with your hands. The dough should be very stiff. Add more flour if needed.

Roll the dough to $\frac{1}{4}$-inch (0.6-cm) thickness on a lightly floured surface. Cut out biscuits with your favorite cookie cutters and place on lightly greased cookie sheets. Repeat rolling and cutting process until all dough is used.

Bake for 40 minutes. Turn off the oven and let the biscuits rest in the oven until hard (about 1 hour).

Store in an airtight container.

YIELD: About 36 cookies (depending on size of cookie cutters)

■

Sugar was developed for the human palate and is not necessary for dogs. Therefore, I recommend using unsweetened applesauce because it contains no sugars (corn syrup or others).

Garlic Herb Biscuits

INGREDIENTS

- 2 cups (250 g) whole wheat flour
- ½ cup (125 g) cornmeal (white or yellow)
- 1 cup (125 g) unbleached flour
- 1 egg, slightly beaten
- 2 tablespoons (30 ml) canola oil (or use your favorite oil)
- 3 garlic cloves, minced
- 1 cup (235 ml) water or chicken broth
- ¼ cup (15 g) parsley, freshly minced or dried

DIRECTIONS

Preheat oven to 350°F (180°C).

In a large bowl, combine dry ingredients. Add the egg, oil, garlic, and liquid, mixing until well blended. Add parsley and mix well. The dough will be stiff. Add more flour if necessary.

On a lightly floured surface, knead the dough and roll out to ¼-inch (0.6-cm) thickness. Using cookie cutters, cut into desired shapes. Repeat rolling and cutting until dough is used.

Place biscuits on a lightly greased baking sheet and bake for 40 minutes. Turn off oven and let biscuits harden inside oven for about 1 hour.

Store biscuits in a sealed container.

YIELD: About 36 large or 60 small biscuits

■

Garlic: To use or not to use—that is the question. Garlic is in the onion family and therefore some veterinarians feel it belongs on the "no-no" list. Holistic veterinarians, however, view garlic as a natural flea repellent and recommend it for medicinal purposes. If you're in doubt, check with your own vet before including this ingredient.

"Stop and smell the flowers, and give me another treat. You love me. You really, really love me."

Carob Chip Cookies

INGREDIENTS

- ¾ cup (60 g) whole rolled oats
- 2 cups (250 g) whole wheat flour (or substitute rye flour)
- 1 cup (260 g) all-natural peanut butter
- 1 cup (235 ml) milk
- ¼ cup (45 g) carob chips, unsweetened

DIRECTIONS

Preheat oven to 375°F (190°C).

In a large bowl, combine oats and flour.

In another bowl, combine peanut butter and milk. Add peanut butter mixture to dry mixture and blend well. Fold in carob chips.

On a lightly floured surface, knead the dough and roll out to ¼-inch (0.6-cm) thickness. Using cookie cutters, cut into desired shapes. Repeat rolling and cutting until all dough is used.

Place biscuits on a lightly greased baking sheet and bake for 25 minutes. Cool on a rack.

Store biscuits in a sealed container.

YIELD: About 55 small cookies

■

Down to the last small bit of dough? Place the dough between palms of hands and roll into fat and thin "noodles" of varying lengths.

"A rose for you, and a cookie for me."

Vegetable Beef Biscuits

INGREDIENTS

- 1 1/4 cups (300 ml) water
- 3/4 cup (90 g) shredded carrots
- one 2 1/2 ounce (70 g) jar beef baby food (or substitute chicken)
- 2 tablespoons (30 ml) canola oil (or use your favorite oil)
- 2 eggs
- 2 tablespoons (8 g) chopped fresh parsley
- 3 1/2 cups (435 g) whole wheat flour
- 3 1/2 cups (435 g) unbleached flour

DIRECTIONS

Preheat oven to 300°F (150°C).

Lightly oil a baking sheet.

In a large bowl, combine water, carrots, beef, oil, and eggs and mix until well blended. Mix together parsley and flours until well blended and add to ingredients in bowl. Mix or knead until well blended.

On a lightly floured area, turn out dough and knead until thoroughly combined. Roll dough to 1/4-inch (0.6-cm) thickness and cut out shapes using cookie cutters. Repeat rolling and cutting until all dough is used. Place cutouts on prepared baking sheet.

Bake 35 minutes. Turn off oven and let biscuits harden in oven until cool.

Cool and store in a sealed container.

YIELD: About 70 biscuits (depending on cutter size and shape)

All breeds and the lovable mutts will agree that a biscuit made with real beef is truly doggie-licious.

Smoochie Poochie Kisses

INGREDIENTS

- 2 cups (250 g) whole wheat flour
- ½ cup (125 g) wheat germ
- ½ cup (120 ml) water
- 1 egg, slightly beaten
- ¼ cup (60 ml) vegetable oil
- 1 tablespoon (8 g) minced mint, dried
- 1 tablespoon (8 g) minced parsley, dried

DIRECTIONS

Preheat oven to 375°F (190°C).

In a medium bowl, stir together flour and wheat germ.

In another bowl, stir together the water, egg, and oil. Combine the wet mixture with the flour mixture. Mix in mint and parsley.

On a lightly floured surface, knead the dough and roll out to ¼-inch (0.6-cm) thickness. Cut out biscuits with favorite small cookie cutter (e.g., a small heart-shaped cutter). Repeat rolling and cutting to use up all the dough.

Place on a lightly greased baking sheet and bake 45 minutes.

Turn off oven and let biscuits harden and cool in oven for 1 hour.

YIELD: 60 small cookies

Mugsy says . . .

These little mint cookies make a great parting gift. If a small heart-shaped cutter is unavailable, have your parent cut out ¾-inch (2-cm) squares.

Get lost in the moment. Everyone loves a kiss.

Granola Biscuits

INGREDIENTS

- 1½ cups (350 ml) water
- 2 tablespoons (30 ml) canola oil (or use your favorite oil)
- 2 eggs, slightly beaten
- 1 cup (250 g) granola
- 4½ cups (560 g) whole wheat flour
- 1 cup (80 g) whole rolled oats

DIRECTIONS

Preheat oven to 350°F (180°C).

In large bowl, combine water, oil, and eggs.

In a second bowl, combine granola, flour, and oats. Add the dry ingredients to the water mixture and mix thoroughly until well blended.

On a lightly floured surface, roll out dough to ¼-inch (0.6-cm) thickness. Using cookie cutters, cut into desired shapes. Repeat rolling and cutting until all dough is used.

Place biscuits on a greased baking sheet and bake for 35 minutes. Turn off oven and let harden inside oven for 30 minutes. Cool on a rack before serving.

Store biscuits in a sealed container.

YIELD: About 60 biscuits (depending on cutter size and shape)

Honey (and/or granola containing honey) can be tricky to bake with because honey tends to burn in the oven, resulting in a dark biscuit. Be sure to tell your parents to adjust the time and temperature according to their oven.

Mugsy says...

While most of us enjoy the chewy, sweet texture and flavor of raisins, some of us have suffered kidney failure after consuming *large* quantities of raisins. The small quantities ordinarily found in granola mix should not cause us any harm, but just to be safe, tell you parent to choose granola without raisins or to pick out the raisins before adding the granola to the recipe.

Biscuits aren't just for breakfast any-
more. When you bake these cookies,
the aroma will have everyone gathering
around the kitchen. Watch out—here
come the neighbors!

Sweet Potato Treats

INGREDIENTS

- 1 large sweet potato
- ¼ cup (60 ml) vegetable oil
- ⅛ cup (28 ml) honey
- 1 egg, slightly beaten
- 1 cup (125 g) unbleached flour

DIRECTIONS

Preheat oven to 350°F (180°C).

Bake sweet potato in oven for about 30 minutes. Cool, peel, and cut potato into 1-inch (2.5-cm) cubes.

In a mixing bowl, combine oil and honey. Add egg and potato and mix thoroughly. Add flour and mix well.

Drop spoonfuls of this wet mixture onto a lightly greased baking sheet.

Bake for 20 minutes. Cool on a rack.

Store in sealed container in refrigerator.

YIELD: 15 to 20 treats

One potato, two potato, three potato, four. Give us Sweet Potato Treats and then give us some more!!

Low-Fat Veggie Biscuits

I call this our hypoallergenic treat, but only if our furry friend is not allergic to any of these ingredients.

INGREDIENTS

- 4 cups (500 g) rye flour
- 1½ cups (120 g) whole rolled oats
- 1 cup (235 ml) water
- 2 eggs, slightly beaten
- ¾ cup (90 g) shredded carrots
- ¼ cup (15 g) freshly minced or dried parsley
- 2 garlic cloves, minced

DIRECTIONS

Preheat oven to 350°F (180°C).

In a medium bowl, stir together flour, oats, and water until well blended. Stir in eggs and add carrots. Add parsley and garlic.

On a lightly floured surface (using rye flour), knead dough (adding more flour if sticky) and roll out to ⅛-inch (0.3-cm) thickness. Cut out ½-inch (1.3 cm) biscuits using pizza cutter or sharp knife.

Place on lightly greased baking sheet and bake for 25 minutes.

Cool and store in a sealed container in the refrigerator.

YIELD: 48 to 60 treats

Don't tell the canine kids that these goodies are low fat—that's our little secret.

CHAPTER 6

Celebration Cakes

Why celebrate? Adoption day. Birthday. Holiday. Graduation. Bark-mitzvah. Bow vows. Agility triumph. Fly-ball championship. Feast of Saint Francis of Assisi pet blessing. Changes of season. And just because! But wait. There's more. Puppy shower. Bone voyage—saying good-bye to a longtime friend who is leaving the neighborhood. A simple "wake" celebrating the life of a dearly departed furry friend who has gone to the Rainbow Bridge. The return of dog parents from a long holiday (without canine kids). A great report from a veterinarian visit.

With all these pawty possibilities just waiting to be celebrated, why not rise to the occasion and bake a cake or mutt muffin? It will surely be spectacular. Happy, happy! Congratulations and watch out for the puparazzi!

Apple Crunch Cake

INGREDIENTS

Cake

- ¾ cup (180 g) unsweetened applesauce
- ¾ cup (175 ml) hot water
- 1 cup (80 g) whole rolled oats
- 3 eggs
- ½ cup (100 g) vegetable shortening
- 1½ teaspoons (3.5 g) cinnamon
- 2 cups (250 g) unbleached flour
- ½ cup (40 g) granola

Frosting (makes 2 cups [400 g])

- ½ cup (100 g) vegetable shortening
- 16 ounces (450 g) cream cheese, softened to room temperature
- 3 tablespoons (24 g) carob powder, divided
- ½ cup (90 g) carob chips, unsweetened
- ¼ teaspoon (3 ml) canola oil

Mugsy says...

Want to create a unique-shaped cake but your parent can't locate a pan? Draw a design on parchment paper or wax paper, trim off the extra paper, place the design on the cooled cake, and trim off the extra cake using a table knife. The excess pieces of cake make great snacking treats.

Your dog's entourage will happily gather around and yap "Yappy Barkday" when you serve this Apple Crunch Cake with a paw-licking good cream cheese frosting. Don't forget the party hats.

continued on the next page >

DIRECTIONS

Cake

Preheat oven to 350°F (180°C).

Lightly spray and flour 9-inch (22.5-cm) square cake pan or desired mold shape.

Combine applesauce, water, and rolled oats and let stand 15 minutes. Blend in the remaining ingredients.

Transfer batter to prepared pan. (The consistency will be thick.) Smooth and flatten batter using spatula.

Bake cake until top is golden, about 40 minutes.

Cool for 10 minutes. Cut around pan sides and remove.

Cool cake completely on a cake rack before frosting.

Frosting

Beat vegetable shortening and cream cheese in a medium bowl until smooth.

For dog bones, place ½ cup (100 g) of mixture in a plastic sandwich bag to remain white.

Blend 2 tablespoons (16 g) carob powder into remainder of frosting until completely blended. Set aside ½ cup (100 g) frosting. Spread remaining frosting over the cake, working down around sides.

Using a toothpick, write your dog's name in the frosting.

Apply stencil design around the name on the cake.

To decorate your cake with dog bones, snip the corner of the sandwich bag and gently squeeze frosting onto cake in the shape of bones.

Combine carob chips and oil in a microwave-safe bowl and heat for 1 minute at 50 percent power. (You are melting the chips; not cooking them.) Remove from microwave and stir until smooth. Transfer to plastic sandwich bag. Snip corner. Gently squeeze bag onto stenciled name on cake.

In small bowl, combine reserved frosting with 1 tablespoon (8 g) carob powder. Place in sandwich bag and squeeze darker frosting along the top edges of the cake to create a border.

If desired, coat half of small biscuits in melted carob and allow the carob to harden.

Decorate cake with biscuits.

Refrigerate cake at least 1 hour before serving.

To eliminate the use of melted carob, you can also write my name on the cake by squeezing some of the prepared white frosting over the "written" name.

Mugsy says...

To create a paw-print stencil on the cake, simply cut out the desired-size print and place it on the cake. Use a fine sieve to lightly dust carob powder onto the cake, then carefully the lift stencil from the cake.

I think this cake tastes even
better when served up with
a drizzle of melted carob.

Mugsy says...

Here's a perfect pawty-favor idea:
grease and flour six 4 $\frac{1}{2}$ x 2 $\frac{1}{2}$ x
1 $\frac{1}{2}$-inch (11 x 6 x 4-cm) loaf pans.
Pour the batter into the pans
and bake for 40–45 minutes. Let
cool, then wrap in colorful wrap
and ribbon to create individual
portions for each guest!

Sweet Potato
(Please Don't Call it "Pound") Cake

INGREDIENTS

- 2 cups (450 g) cooked, cooled, and mashed sweet potato
- 1 teaspoon (5 ml) vanilla
- ½ cup (100 ml) honey
- 4 eggs
- ½ cup (100 g) vegetable shortening
- 3 cups (380 g) unbleached flour
- 2 teaspoons (9.2 g) baking powder
- ½ teaspoon (2.3 g) baking soda
- 2 teaspoons (5 g) cinnamon
- ½ teaspoon (1.2 g) nutmeg

DIRECTIONS

Preheat oven to 350°F (180°C).

Grease a 10-inch (25-cm) tube pan.

In a large bowl, beat together potatoes, vanilla, and honey until well blended. Add the eggs, one at a time, beating 1 minute for each egg. Add the shortening and beat until well combined.

In another bowl, mix together flour, baking powder, baking soda, cinnamon, and nutmeg. Slowly add the flour mixture to the sweet potato mixture. Beat on slow speed until combined. Pour batter into the prepared pan.

Bake for 60–70 minutes.

Cool cake and serve in thin slices.

Store in sealed container in refrigerator.

YIELD: 20 servings (depending on size of guests)

■

To cook sweet potatoes, wash, peel, and cut the potatoes into quarters. Cook, covered, in boiling water for 25 minutes. Drain and rinse until smooth.

"Correct me if I'm wrong, but don't I get seven birthdays per year?"

Mama's Magic Mutt Muffins

These muffins are tasty, and the mild apple flavor will entice even the pickiest of pups. Magic? Oh yeah. Watch them disappear.

INGREDIENTS

- 2 cups (250 g) unbleached flour
- 3 teaspoons (5 g) cinnamon, divided
- 1 teaspoon (4.6 g) baking powder
- ½ teaspoon (2.3 g) baking soda
- 2 eggs
- ¼ cup (60 ml) vegetable oil
- 1 cup (230 g) plain low-fat yogurt
- 1 cup (150 g) peeled, finely chopped apples

DIRECTIONS

Preheat oven to 400°F (200°C).

Lightly grease 12 muffin cups.

In a large bowl, stir together flour, cinnamon, baking powder, and baking soda.

In a smaller bowl, beat the eggs, then stir in oil and yogurt. Add egg mixture to flour mixture. Stir in apples until just moistened.

Spoon batter into muffin cups to about ⅔ full. Sprinkle tops with remaining 1 teaspoon (1.6 g) cinnamon.

Bake for 20–25 minutes.

Cool and store in sealed container in refrigerator.

YIELD: 12 muffins

These pups must be dreaming about the day they can have Mama's Magic Mutt Muffins with their milk.

Blueberry Muffins

These muffins are perfect for a midmorning snack. They will pep up your pup with a boost of energy.

INGREDIENTS

- 1 ¾ cups (220 g) unbleached flour
- 2 ½ teaspoons (11.5 g) baking powder
- 1 egg, slightly beaten
- ¾ cup (175 ml) milk
- ⅓ cup (80 ml) vegetable oil
- ¼ cup (60 ml) honey
- 1 cup (145 g) blueberries

DIRECTIONS

Preheat oven to 375°F (190°C).

Lightly grease 9 muffin cups.

In a small bowl, stir together flour and baking powder.

In a large bowl, stir together the egg, milk, oil, and honey. Add flour mixture to egg mixture. Fold in blueberries. Spoon batter into muffin cups to about ⅔ full.

Bake for 25 minutes.

Cool and store in sealed container in refrigerator.

YIELD: 9 muffins

Mugsy says...

If fresh blueberries are unavailable, I also like frozen blueberries! They are easier to fold into the batter without bursting, too.

"Surely if I return this ball to my canine parents, they'll replace it with a blueberry muffin, right?"

Carrot Muffins with Frosting

INGREDIENTS

Muffins

- 2 cups (250 g) shredded carrots
- 3 eggs
- ½ cup (120 ml) vegetable oil
- 2 teaspoons (5 g) cinnamon
- ½ cup (40 g) whole rolled oats
- 3 cups (375 g) unbleached flour

Frosting (makes 1 cup [200 g])

- 8 ounces (230 g) cream cheese, softened to room temperature
- ¼ cup (50 g) vegetable shortening

DIRECTIONS

Muffins

Preheat oven to 300°F (150°C).

Lightly grease 9 muffin cups.

Combine carrots, eggs, and oil until well blended. Slowly add cinnamon, oats, and flour to mixture until well blended.

"Shape" muffins with hands and place into muffin pans. Wet hands with water to make this step easier.

Bake 25 minutes.

Cool completely before frosting.

Frosting

Blend ingredients with a hand mixer until well blended.

Place frosting in a pastry bag with an easy "flower" tip, or a large plastic sandwich bag, and pipe a large circle on the perimeter, coming closer to the center in three concentric circles on top of the muffin. You can also spread frosting on the muffins with a spatula.

If desired, garnish with a cookie.

YIELD: 9 muffins

■

Save any leftover frosting and spread between two biscuits to make canine sandwich cookies.

Carrot muffins never tasted so good! These muffins can be divided into eight portions and make great training aids.

Grandma Sadie's Apple Pancake

This recipe is literally a pancake. This is an old-fashioned dessert that never goes out of style—especially doggie style.

INGREDIENTS

- 2 tablespoons (25 g) vegetable shortening or oil
- 2 Red or Golden Delicious apples, peeled, cored, and thinly sliced
- 1 teaspoon (2.5 g) cinnamon
- ⅓ cup (50 g) walnuts, finely chopped
- ⅓ cups (40 g) unbleached flour
- ¼ teaspoon (1.15 g) baking powder
- 2 eggs, separated
- ⅓ cup (80 ml) milk

DIRECTIONS

Preheat oven to 400°F (200°C).

In a 10-inch (25-cm) skillet with an oven-safe handle, melt the shortening. Add apples and cinnamon, stir to coat well, cover, and cook on low heat for 5 minutes. Remove from heat and add walnuts.

In a medium bowl, combine flour, baking powder, egg yolks, and milk. Beat until the batter is smooth.

In a medium bowl, using an electric hand mixer, beat the egg whites until soft peaks form. Gently fold egg white mixture into flour mixture. Pour the batter over the apples and nuts in the skillet.

Bake in oven for 15 minutes. Remove from oven and gently loosen the edges of the pancake with a spatula.

Place a serving plate over the skillet and turn over (apples will be on top).

YIELD: 12 servings (depending on the size of the portions)

Mugsy says...

Grandma served this recipe with ice cream to the kids. For us dogs, spoon a bit of plain low-fat yogurt on top as a yummy garnish.

Cranberry Nut Bars

These chewy delights are not only tasty, they're healthy, too! Our canine friends love cranberries. Team them up with oats and who knows, you'll probably try one yourself. Bone appetit!

INGREDIENTS

- 1½ cups (350 ml) water
- ¼ cup (60 ml) honey
- 3 cups (330 g) cranberries, fresh or frozen
- ½ cup (100 g) vegetable shortening
- ½ teaspoon (2.3 g) baking soda
- ½ teaspoon (1.3 g) cinnamon
- 1½ cups (180 g) unbleached flour
- 1¼ cups (125 g) whole rolled oats
- ½ cup (75 g) walnuts, finely chopped

DIRECTIONS

Preheat oven to 375°F (190°C).

Lightly grease a 13 x 9 x 2-inch (33 x 23 x 5-cm) baking pan.

In a medium saucepan, combine water and honey and bring to a boil. Add cranberries and return to a boil. Reduce heat and boil gently for 10 minutes, stirring occasionally. Remove from heat and cool slightly.

In a large bowl, cream the shortening and add baking soda and cinnamon. Slowly add flour, about ½ cup (60 g) at a time. Stir in oats. (The mixture will be crumbly.) Divide the flour mixture in half and press one half evenly into baking pan.

Spread cranberry mixture evenly over flour mixture. Spread chopped walnuts evenly over cranberry mixture. Sprinkle with remaining flour mixture, gently pressing into the bottom layer.

Bake for 25 minutes. Cool on a wire rack.

Cut into bars.

YIELD: 20 to 25 bars

Carob Chip Muffins

INGREDIENTS

- 1½ cups (345 g) plain low-fat yogurt
- 3 eggs, slightly beaten
- ½ cup (100 g) vegetable shortening
- ¼ cup (32 g) carob powder
- 4 cups (500 g) unbleached flour
- ½ cup (40 g) whole rolled oats
- ¼ cup (45 g) unsweetened carob chips

DIRECTIONS

Preheat oven to 300°F (150°C).

Lightly grease 9 muffin cups.

In mixer bowl, combine yogurt, eggs, and shortening until well blended.

In another bowl, combine carob powder, flour, and oats until well blended. Add dry ingredients to the yogurt mixture and blend thoroughly. Stir in carob chips.

"Shape" muffins with hands and place into muffin pans. Wet hands with water to make this step easier.

Bake 25 minutes.

Cool and store in a sealed container in refrigerator.

YIELD: 9 muffins

"Chocolate" for dogs? Doggie-safe carob is a Mediterranean pod plant that is truly doggie-licious!

Sweet Potato Muffins

The naturally sweet sweet potato makes these muffins ideal for training. Break into little pieces and start to train away!

INGREDIENTS

- 1 sweet potato
- 3 eggs, slightly beaten
- ½ cup (100 g) vegetable shortening
- 1½ teaspoons (3.5 g) cinnamon
- 1½ teaspoons (3.5 g) ground ginger
- 2 cups (250 g) unbleached flour
- 1 cup (80 g) whole rolled oats

DIRECTIONS

Preheat oven to 300°F (150°C).

Lightly grease 9 muffin cups.

Bake sweet potato for 45 minutes. Allow potato to cool, then peel and mash.

In a large bowl, combine potato, eggs, and shortening.

In a medium bowl, combine cinnamon, ginger, flour, and oats. Add flour mixture to potato mixture and blend well.

Spoon batter into prepared muffin pan.

Bake for 30 minutes.

Cool for 10 minutes. Remove muffins from pan and cool completely on a wire rack.

Cool and store in a sealed container in the refrigerator.

YIELD: 9 regular muffins or 12 mini muffins

Pumpkin Brownies

INGREDIENTS

Brownie

- ½ cup (100 g) vegetable shortening
- 2 eggs, slightly beaten
- 2 cups (250 g) unbleached flour
- 2 teaspoons (9.2 g) baking powder
- 2 teaspoons (5 g) cinnamon
- 1 cup (225 g) puréed pumpkin
- ¾ cup (175 ml) milk

Frosting

- 8 ounces (230 g) cream cheese, softened to room temperature
- ½ cup (100 g) vegetable shortening

DIRECTIONS

Brownie

Preheat oven to 350°F (180°C).

Lightly grease a 9 x 9 x 2-inch (23 x 23 x 5-cm) baking pan.

In a large bowl, cream the shortening. Beat in eggs.

In a medium bowl, mix together flour, baking powder, and cinnamon. Add pumpkin and milk. Mix thoroughly.

Add the pumpkin mixture to the shortening mixture and blend well. Pour into greased pan.

Bake for 40–45 minutes. Cool in the pan on a wire rack. Remove from pan and cool completely.

Frosting

Cream shortening and beat in cream cheese. Spread frosting over cooled brownies. Cut into squares.

Cool and store in a sealed container in refrigerator.

YIELD: 40 to 44 brownies, 1½-inch (3.8-cm) in size

■

To wowie-zowie these brownies up, add ½ cup (75 g) chopped walnuts to the batter. For the carobholics, fold ½ cup (90 g) unsweetened carob chips into the batter.

Mugsy says...

I love it when my parent uses the leftover frosting as the center for two brownies. Yummmmm.

CHAPTER 7

Chilled Tarts &
Beverages

Keep the momentum of your canine celebration going by taking it over the top with chilled desserts, "muttgaritas," and doggie daiquiris. Everyone will surely give a high paw for one of these chilled delights. Because all the following recipes are temperature-sensitive, they must remain chilled until served. If your soirée is in the park, remember to keep these recipes packed in coolers with plenty of ice.

You can add a touch of whimsy by accenting these treats with theme-inspired goodies and décor. We all have memories of cakes and special pies or tarts—let your canines create their own special memories with these chilled tarts and goodies!

Doggie Daiquiri

INGREDIENTS

- 2 cups (450 g) plain low-fat yogurt
- 1 tablespoon (15 ml) water
- 2 tablespoons (30 g) puréed pumpkin

DIRECTIONS

Using hand mixer, combine ingredients in small bowl until well blended.

Freeze for 1 hour, stirring every 15 minutes, then serve.

NOTE: This treat must be frozen or refrigerated until served.

■

This drink goes well with the Pumpkin Twists found on page 84.

■

Be a creative bark-tender and design your own doggie daiquiri. Instead of pumpkin, try using 2 tablespoons (30 g) peanut butter and 2 tablespoons (30 g) mashed banana or half a jar of any flavor baby food that appeals to your dog.

YIELD: 2 cups (475 ml)

Mugsy says ...

During the summer months, serve me a refreshing treat by placing the yogurt mixture in ice cube trays and freezing individual portions.

It's five o'clock somewhere. Let the Yappy Hour gets started with a refreshing chilled pumpkin Doggie Daiquiri.

Bananarita

INGREDIENTS

- 4 cups (920 g) plain low-fat yogurt
- 2 tablespoons (40 g) raw honey (optional)
- 1 sliced banana

DIRECTIONS

Mix all ingredients in a blender or food processor. Freeze in ice cube trays or a favorite mold.

Release creams from trays into a serving bowl and keep chilled until ready to serve.

YIELD: 4 cups (946 ml)

■

Personal favorites really come into play with this basic recipe. Add whatever fruit or vegetables your dog prefers. A few suggestions include blueberries, cranberries, pumpkin, carrots, puréed butternut squash, and apples. Yogurt is very good for your dog, as it aids digestion. To tempt even the pickiest eater, add a little puréed beef, lamb, chicken, venison, or salmon.

A favorite trick at my house is to place this treat in the freezer, scrape off the top of the cream with a fork every thirty minutes to form crystals, and serve the crystals on party plates.

Mugsy says...

Peanut butter is one of my favorite sources of protein. Tell your parent to be creative and add ¼ cup (65 g) of all-natural peanut butter to the yogurt. For a nutritional boost, add 1 tablespoon (6 g) flaxseed meal.

No booties? No collars? No problem. Transport your guests to the tropical latitudes with these refreshingly cool treats.

above:
These yummy cups are really two treats in one ... a crunchy cookie and a smooth pumpkin filling. Make it three by topping it off with a cookie.

left:
If you're not handy with a pastry bag and assorted tips, fill a sandwich bag with your frosting mixture, snip the corner edge, and squeeze the mixture into the cups. Smooth the filling with a knife or your finger.

Pumpkin Cheese Cups

INGREDIENTS

Cookie Cups

- 2 1/2 cups (310 g) whole wheat flour
- 1/2 cup (40 g) whole rolled oats
- 1 egg, slightly beaten
- 1 cup (240 ml) water
- 1/2 cup (130 g) all-natural crunchy peanut butter

Filling

- 1/2 cup (100 g) puréed pumpkin
- 16 ounces (450 g) cream cheese, softened to room temperature

DIRECTIONS

Cookie Cups

Preheat oven to 350°F (180°C).

Combine wheat flour and oats in a large bowl. Add egg, water, and peanut butter and mix well.

On a lightly floured surface, knead the dough and roll out to 1/8-inch (0.3-cm) thickness. Cut out twenty-four 2-inch (5-cm) circles. Use remaining dough to cut out 24 small garnish cookies.

Spray a mini muffin pan with oil and lightly dust with flour. Lay cookie circles in the mini muffin cups and press.

Bake 30 minutes or until golden brown. Cool enough to handle, remove from pan, then let cool completely.

Store in sealed container until ready to fill with cheese mixture.

Filling

With a hand mixer, mix pumpkin and cream cheese together until well blended. Place cream cheese mixture into a pastry bag with a large tip opening or a plastic sandwich bag. Snip corner of sandwich baggie to create a 1/2-inch (1.3 cm) opening. Gently squeeze filling into cookie cups.

Garnish with a small cookie.

YIELD: About 24 mini mutt cups and 24 garnish cookies

Mugsy says...

Here's an idea: cut out my favorite cookie shapes from the leftover dough to garnish the top of each cheese-filled cup.

Ooh La La Peanut Butter Pie

INGREDIENTS

Crust

- 1½ cups (190 g) unbleached flour
- ½ cup (100 g) vegetable shortening
- 1 teaspoon (2.5 g) cinnamon
- 4–5 tablespoons (60–75 ml) cold water

Filling

- 1½ tablespoons (12 g) unbleached flour
- 1 cup (235 ml) milk
- 2 egg yolks
- 1 cup (260 g) peanut butter
- 1 tablespoon (4 g) minced mint, plus whole-leaf mint for garnish

DIRECTIONS

Crust

Preheat oven to 450°F (230°C).

Sift flour into a medium bowl. Cut in shortening until dough forms ¼-inch (0.6-cm) balls. Sprinkle in cinnamon. Sprinkle in 1 tablespoon (15 ml) water at a time over mixture and gently toss with a fork until crust forms into a ball. Flatten pastry ball on a lightly floured surface.

Roll out pastry to ⅛-inch (3-mm) thickness. Cut out five 6-inch (15-cm) crust rounds. Fit into 4-inch (10-cm) mini pie plates and trim excess.

Bake 10–12 minutes and cool.

Filling

Place all ingredients in a blender and blend until smooth.

Pour into a saucepan and cook over medium heat until mixture thickens. Do not let the mixture boil.

Cool and pour into pie shell(s). Refrigerate until set.

Before serving, stencil on a paw print or garnish with a bit of cream cheese and fresh mint.

YIELD: Five 4-inch (10-cm) pies or one 8-inch (20-cm) pie

Naturally sweet, the sweet potato pie (next page, shown top) is paws-down irresistible—from the crunchy tart to the smooth filling. A dollop of smooth cream cheese "frosting" will take this tasty tart over the top! The peanut butter pie (bottom) is the most direct route to a peanut butter fix this side of a spoon. The guests will sniff for more. This tart can be divided into four servings or more.

Sweet Paw-tato Pie

INGREDIENTS

Crust

- 1½ cups (190 g) unbleached flour
- ⅓ cup (70 g) vegetable shortening
- 1 teaspoon (2.5 g) cinnamon
- 3–4 tablespoons (45–60 ml) ice water

Filling

- 1 large sweet potato
- 1 egg
- ½ teaspoon (1.3 g) cinnamon

DIRECTIONS

Crust

Preheat oven to 350°F (180°C).

Sift flour into a medium bowl. Cut in shortening until dough forms ¼-inch (0.6-cm) balls. Sprinkle in cinnamon. Sprinkle in 1 tablespoon (15 ml) water at a time over mixture and gently toss with a fork until crust forms into a ball. Flatten pastry ball on a lightly floured surface.

Roll out pastry to ⅛-inch (3-mm) thickness. Cut out five 4-inch (10-cm) crust rounds. Fit into 4-inch (10-cm) mini pie plates and trim excess.

Filling

Bake sweet potato for 30 minutes. Cool and peel.

In a medium bowl, mix potato, egg, and cinnamon until smooth. Pour potato mixture into crusts and bake 25 minutes.

Cool tart before serving.

If desired, garnish with cream cheese and a carob chip.

Wrap with film and store in refrigerator.

YIELD: Five 4-inch (10-cm) pies or one 8-inch (20-cm) pie

Carob Cheese Tart

INGREDIENTS

Crust

- 1 1/2 cups (190 g) unbleached flour
- 1 tablespoon (8 g) carob powder
- 2 cups (400 g) vegetable shortening
- 4–5 tablespoons (60–75 ml) ice water

Filling

- 8 ounces (230 g) cream cheese, softened to room temperature
- 1 egg, slightly beaten
- 1/2 cup (90 g) carob chips, unsweetened
- 1 teaspoon (5 ml) vanilla
- 1/2 cup (115 g) plain low-fat yogurt

DIRECTIONS

Crust

Preheat oven to 350°F (180°C).

Lightly grease five 4-inch (10-cm) mini pie plates.

In a medium bowl, sift flour and carob powder. Cut in shortening until dough forms 1/4-inch (0.6-cm) balls. Sprinkle in 1 tablespoon (15 ml) water at a time over mixture and gently toss with a fork until crust forms into ball. Flatten pastry ball on a lightly floured surface.

Roll out dough to 1/8-inch (0.3 cm) thickness. Cut out five 6-inch (15-cm) crust rounds. Fit into 4-inch (10-cm) mini pie plates, trim, and set aside.

Filling

In a large bowl, combine the cream cheese and egg and blend until the mixture is smooth.

In a medium bowl, melt carob chips in microwave oven for 1 minute on 50 percent power. Stir in vanilla and yogurt. Beat the warm carob mixture into the cream cheese mixture.

Spoon the filling into the pie plates. Level off tops with a rubber spatula.

Bake for about 60 minutes. Remove from oven and cool for 2 hours.

Cut into pieces and serve.

YIELD: About 20 servings

■

These luscious cheese tarts can be frozen for later soirées.

Carob Frappe

This is a refreshing "mocktail" for any pawty! Serve slightly frozen or right out of the blender.

INGREDIENTS

- ice cubes
- 1 cup (230 g) plain low-fat yogurt
- 1 tablespoon (8 g) carob powder (more if you like)
- 2 tablespoons (30 ml) milk
- 1 tablespoon (7 g) wheat germ
- 1 tablespoon (20 g) honey

DIRECTIONS

Fill a blender half full with ice cubes. Add all ingredients and blend thoroughly. Pour a bit into small bowls and serve.

YIELD: 10 to 15 servings (depending on the size of the guests)

■

These treats can also be served frozen. Simply freeze the mixture, stirring every 10 minutes for about 45 minutes, then spoon onto plates and serve.

Mugsy says...

If I don't sip all this frappe, fill an ice cube tray with the leftovers. I can enjoy a frozen serving later on!

"This is yummy but a Doggie Daiquiri or Carob Frappe would also do the trick."

Resources

Always check with your local animal shelter, rescue groups, or the Yellow Pages for additional resources.

Ann Clark Ltd.
www.annclark.com
Cookie cutters in various shapes and sizes

Barbara's Canine Catering. Inc.
www.k9treat.com
All-natural dog foods and treats, baked goods, doggy gift baskets, birthday cakes, and Muttgaritas

Canine Café Charlotte
Charlotte, North Carolina
888-598-7328
All-natural dog foods and treats, baked goods, doggy gift baskets, birthday cakes, Muttgaritas, pet fashions, outdoor gear, party hats and invitations

Castlemere
www.castlemere.com
sales@castlemere.com
Wholesale pet accessories, bowls, jars, and feeders

Charming Pet Products
www.charmingpetproducts.com
Collar pet charms for dogs and cats

Dog Rescue Organizations
www.akc.org
www.petfinders.org
www.rescuers.com

Frontier Natural products Co-Op
www.frontiercoop.com
Specialty grains, flour, herbs, and spices

nycake.com
www.nycake.com
Cake decorating, baking, and pastry supplies

Off the Beaten Path
www.cookiecutter.com
Cookie cutters in various shapes and sizes

Pet Rageous Pet Products
www.petrageousdesigns.com
Bowls, feeders, treat jars, placemats, mugs, and more

Pet Studio
www.petedge.com
Professional pet products and pet supplies for dog grooming, dog training, kennels, dog breeding, and veterinarians; available at pet stores

Piedmont Pets
www.piedmontpets.com
Leather collars and leashes, organic catnip, cat toys, show bows, pet treats, and gourmet bones

Tropical Nut & Fruit
www.tropicalnutandfruit.com
Baking supplies and ingredients

About the Author

Barbara Burg, a North Carolina native, attended both the University of North Carolina (UNC) and East Carolina University, where she received a B.F.A. degree. After graduating, she moved to New York City and launched a Broadway career. She performed in professional theater in Manhattan and with national touring companies before moving to Los Angeles, where she met her husband, Andrew. In 1994 they relocated to Charlotte, North Carolina, and established Barbara's Canine Catering the following year. Barbara has been baking treats, snacks, and cakes for dogs ever since, with the goal of developing recipes to embrace the holistic, all-natural lifestyle. After years of success with the dog bakery, Barbara and her husband (along with business partners David and Meredith Thompson Greer) went on to create Canine Café Charlotte in 2004.

Barbara is active in animal rescue organizations throughout the Carolinas and is a strong supporter of the Los Cabos Humane Society in Baja, Mexico. She has been featured on Animal Planet, the Food Network's *Extreme Cuisine*, and Fox Network's *Pet Department*. Her cakes have been featured on ABC-TV's *Good Morning America*. In addition to running the day-to-day business, Barbara teaches private seminars designed to help other dog lovers start their own dog bakeries and retail businesses.

Dedication

In loving memory of my mother, Mildred, who supported my love of baking for dogs and who so enthusiastically supported the development of Barbara's Canine Catering.

To my father, Cecil, my best friend, whose love and support keeps me going in my quest to bake the healthiest treats available for our canine kids.

My father, Cecil, who occasionally dressed up Sparky to go out and about, circa 1946. After seeing this photograph, it became very clear to me where I got the gene for wanting to party with dogs.

Photographer Credits

Recipe photographs by Donna Bise
Donna Bise earned a degree in journalism from the University of South Carolina. As an award-winning photojournalist for more than twenty years, she has photographed people on location for corporate and editorial clients across the U.S., Europe, Asia, and Central America. She makes her home with her family in Charlotte, North Carolina.

Courtesy of Mary Aarons, 15 (top)

Mugsy photograph courtesy of Linda Fund

Courtesy of Chris Grimley, 70

Courtesy of Alison Peterson, 7 (left)

Ande Abramovich, 55

All other photography, with the exception of Cecil's portrait, page 140 www.istock.com.

Food styling by Teresa Chelko

Acknowledgments

As I write these words, TJ is fourteen and a half years old. He's a bit slower, crankier, and more stubborn but still sharp and alert. He's also very particular about which treats are his favorites. This book is as much a tribute to his long and vibrant life as anyone or anything else. He was the inspiration. He was the reason. He was the storefront supermarket rescue puppy, just six weeks old, days before Christmas 1992, saved by my good friend Lori Koppel-Heath. What a wonderful gift you provided me, Lori. All of us were blessed by his presence on this earth, and by the many years of joy he brought to our lives. He's lived on both coasts. He's seen mountains, beaches, and deserts. From the tip of Baja to Lake Tahoe, he's enjoyed his travels and all the good cooking along the way. TJ has shared in the development of the treats in this book from start to finish.

A big high paw goes out to Dr. Brawn, D.V.M., who, in 1994, suggested that we take TJ off of most commercial treats and suggested I bake him some homemade treats. I listened. TJ became the corporate CEO (Chief Eating Officer) of Barbara's Canine Catering. And the rest is history.

A big high paw goes out to Andrew Burg, who shared my vision of creating a catering business and all-natural dog treat bakery to provide freshly baked, healthy, wholesome products. Thank you for the countless donated hours developing and growing the "business" of the business. Thank you for the tens of thousands of biscuits you've cut out at the café and years of support to keep it going. Thank you for your dedication in helping type, assemble, edit, proofread, and do metric conversions so that I could get this book completed.

High paws go out to Dr. Kim Robinson, DVM, who has taken such great care of my canine and feline kids and has guided me through the years in many "culinary" decisions, along with Dr. Tom Watson, D.V.M., and the North Carolina State University Food Science Department, without whom I would not have a good foundation for developing all-natural recipes.

A major high paw to business partners David and Meredith Thompson Greer for their shared vision in creating a store where dogs can get products to keep them in the healthy and holistic lifestyle. Thanks for your encouragement and taking care of the business while I've been working on this project. Thanks for creating both a location and an experience for two- and four-legged pawty guests.

High paws go out to the thousands of canines nationwide that enjoy Barbara's Canine Catering products every month and have encouraged us to bake for their special dietary needs.

And thanks to our own taste testers: TJ, Hoover, Taco, Penny, Holli, Andi, Dixie, and the canine customers of Canine Café Charlotte for putting in countless hours of testing these yummies.

And, of course, to those very first customers who were as crazy as me to actually order up a catered canine event and trusted in me to deliver exactly what is described in this book. Thank you, Mary Tribble, for your early vote of confidence in my abilities.

High paws to the baking staff at Barbara's Canine Catering for testing these recipes, especially Claudia, Gloria, Dunia, Miriam, Elijio, Leyci, and Memory.

High paws to Abigail Mace, who at only 10 years old knows the beauty and fulfillment of dog guardianship. She assists us at Canine Café Charlotte on Saturdays during Yappy Hour and wants to become a professional dog handler. Good luck, Abbie. We'll see you at Westminster.

High paws to Donna Bise and Teresa Chelko for your fun and whimsical work with the treats and cakes photographs in this book.

High paws to Canine Café Charlotte for the use of dog bowls, treat jars, dog collars, and party hats and bandanas used in the photographs and provided by our suppliers: Pet-Rageous, Castlemere, Pet Studio, Charming Pet Products, and Piedmont Pets.

Thanks to the media—from magazines and newspapers to television and radio— without whom we could not have succeeded. The media has been good to me. I have been blessed with extensive exposure these past twelve years and that has helped our all-natural dog-treat bakery become a success and provided much-needed financial support to the rescue groups with whom we work.

High paws to Barbara Bourassa, Regina Grenier, Betsy Gammons, and Winnie Prentiss at Quarry Books for your advice and guidance. And lastly, high paws to Candice Janco for recommending me to the publishers for this project. Woof!